Breathing Ashes

Ashes

A Poetic Guide to To Walking Through
The Fire and Coming Out Reborn

Greg Corbin II

Breathing Ashes
is a collection of stories, poems, essays and teachings compiled by Just Greg* from 2005-2020. The opposite of burnout is engagement.

For information contact: *GregCorbinSpeaks@gmail.com*

ISBN: 978-1-7363855-0-0

First Edition

Manufactured in the United States of America

For information regarding special discounts for bulk purchases, please contact Special Sales at Jane.Nicole.Mitchell@gmail.com.

*Greg **R**ises **E**ngaged with **G**ratitude*

This book is dedicated:
To My Mom and Dad.
To the Alchemists.
To the Dream Weavers.

A BREATHING ASHES INTRO

You may be wondering why the title of this book is "Breathing Ashes?" The more I've infused the words "Breathing Ashes" with oxygen the more it becomes clear that the meaning is not in the words, but literally in the perception of it. Shortly after climbing Mt Sinai, where Moses stayed 40 days and 40 nights to receive and create the Ten Commandments, the concept "Breathing Ashes" was born. My Wife and I were sitting by the Red Sea in Sharm El-Sheikh, Egypt discussing how our second honeymoon became a spiritual pilgrimage, **sharing insight on** topics such as the reproductive system, child rearing and rebirth. During this conversation I realized the profound importance of dying many deaths while we are still breathing and stepping into the courage to release the previous versions of who we once were in order to become something even greater.

I once heard a friend say, "I don't know what's wrong with you. I don't even know who you are anymore." I responded, "I don't either, but it's better than repeating the last decade of my life." I found myself in a feedback loop, repeating the same story, attached to similar outcomes, running from moment to moment in the name of comfort. I enjoyed the chaos, stayed addicted to the disorder, claiming the need to wander with no direction other than serving others in the spirit of giving back through philanthropic ventures. Forgetting **how a** person cannot pour from an empty cup, I disregarded the need for reflection and introspection. I wasn't able to put myself in position to identify the wisdom that I gained. By choosing to carry the burden of others while holding their cross stretched across my back I **found myself** crucified by the weight that was never mine to bear. These were my choices to choose and I chose them.

The Bible mentions the "Spiritual Woodshed" as a moment in which an individual has to travel within. And that is what I did. Traveled deep within. There was no roadmap for the journey. Just courageous inner dialogue full of accountability. It was a time of isolation where I, the student, had to study the classroom I created in order to find my way back to myself. And that's just it! Maybe we come to this planet to experience life in human form, purposely getting lost only to find ourselves again. As I traversed through the experience, I explored my light and shadow selves, holding constructive conversations with multiple beings within. Different versions of self that I manifested over the years, each one teaching something new. I learned that inside was actually innerspace, a galaxy of epiphanies and discovery. I learned to turn the struggles into strategy, as I transformed the pain into activated learning and application. I began to rise from the valley of victimhood, reclaiming the power of responsibility as I stepped into a transformation of triumph. I learned the power of moving slow in a fast paced world.

Fire is the great purifier. It is the shaper, the molder, the holder of possibility. I pray you enjoy the rise of flame that I share with you through these writings. Sometimes we have to realize we are the burning building that we have to run into. That we are in need of water. That we need to nurture ourselves, because an individual is unable to pour from an empty cup. If we aren't able to manage the raging fire within, then we can burn anything and anyone that comes near us. We can consume everything with our heat for life. I've decided to burn as much as I can to create ashes. **This book is not an urn, but a compass to help guide you as you discover what ashes you need to create and breathe.** In the spirit of sharing wisdom and experience, I offer an authentic voice in a moment where sharing undisturbed truth is a courageous act, especially when sourced from within. It is time to embrace our inner phoenix. Embracing our transformation for the world is releasing the old and inviting the new.

There is only me. As I am. Just Greg.

Spiritual Healing

On Burnout and Boundaries

Your emotional state is your feeling and it's composition based on the current happenstance of your life. It is filled with the story you've conjured in your mind. It is a story composed of thoughts and ideas of who you are supposed to be or who you are manufactured to be. It's all engineered by a series of myths you've aimed to create your identity from. It's your story. *It's all you.* It's your thinking. *It's all you.* It's your perspective. *It's all you.* It's all in the mind. *As a person thinketh - so they drinketh* from the pool of life. The question remains: what have you chosen to become?

> ## "I've come to find that people are not living life. They are living their perceptions."
> ### - @GregCorbinSpeaks

The best accomplishment a person can have is to find themselves spiritually, because in that way you truly begin to know who you are and why you are. Only you can know that answer. It is your driving force, your graceful truth. No one else can tell you who you are, unless you already are aware of who you are. If you don't know who you are, others will create justifiable personas of who you need to be from their perspective and experience with life. We train people how to treat us, for better or for worse.

At one point, I played the guy who wanted to put out all the fires, operating from a place of desperation and insecurity. I was operating from pain and suffering, developing a savior complex that ignored the idea or person I was creating. Eventually the fires put me out. I was burnt out beyond my own recognition. I was lost in a world designed by my own ego. It was designed around childhood trauma and developmental needs my upbringing didn't have access or resources to. After many conversations I know that I am not alone.

People will buy into what you're selling. It's based upon belief systems. It's no different than a religion and often dependent on how many operational ideologies you have internally. That's how much you're selling. You're a hot commodity when you're selling something many in the population want and desire.

There are many times when a person's jealousy is derived from their own misery. They are envious that they haven't tapped into the power of courage one has in order to achieve and accomplish what they want. (Although sometimes they will find it's not even what they want) Therefore, they will commiserate about a pain body, internal markings of events that still hold them hostage emotionally, mentally and spiritually. They are consumed with how others have failed them. They are simmering in the blame game, unaware that they are giving away their power by thrusting responsibility on someone else.

That was me. Giving away responsibility for how people made me feel. No one can make you feel a certain way. You must allow them to make you feel an emotion. It is your responsibility to manage your emotions.

"You are calling you to you!"
- @GregCorbinSpeaks

Therefore, I stepped back to master the shadows within in order to shine a brighter light - without becoming a supernova. The shadow is the body of insecurities, trauma from life experiences, bad learnings and limited beliefs. It includes non productive stories we've learned about self and negative thoughts. Sometimes there are wounds that only you are in the position to pull back and let breathe. I've had to battle to lift the scab in order for new oxygen to hit the scar. It's taken some time, but these scars are dissolving into a classroom of knowledge of self. It's heightened my awareness and my awareness of others. Behind every shadow is a lesson that is waiting to become wisdom. It's been a challenge that I wouldn't change for nothing. I was programmed to pursue external change and I was ignoring all the beautiful opportunities within to expand and evolve as a human being.

This isn't about self pity, but about being authentically honest and assertive in creating the life I or you want. It's easy to point fingers at the world instead of looking deeply into the development of your mental and emotional climate that is leading to manifest certain results. I'm responsible and no one else.

The human experience is a classroom with no curriculum. Along the journey we must find the tools of expression to process our travels. Through meditation, yoga, and other forms of stillness art, I've been able to reflect, resurrect and alchemize many parts of myself for my highest good. It's taken discipline, consistency, truth seeking practices, and genuine love.

I've mastered chaos and now I'm mastering peace. The world was not designed to bring you peace, you must bring peace to the world. In order for that to occur, you must explore the many ways of chaos that you've internalized, so that you can move differently and etch out a path towards internal peace. The placid lake or still water within is calling your name. You are calling you to you!

Like a conditioned and seasoned firefighter, I ran to put out the flames of others, exhausting the fire that God granted me. I've learned to pace myself, keep better boundaries and to shamelessly exercise them without the ever-haunting *people pleasing* mentality. No. I am not perfect in this. It is still a work in progress.

Burnt out I was; and then it reality hit. I realized the people I thought were there for me were really there for what I could provide. I realized that I was fuel for their fire, and unselfishly gave my energy to them only to find out, it just wasn't fully equitable.

We must constantly evaluate our intention for having certain people in our lives, because everyone isn't worthy of our attention, or energy.

"The lack of self care was my weakness. The lack of self care was my failure. I put so much pressure on myself that I broke myself." - @GregCorbinSpeaks

I've been more purposeful with my life, intentionally stepping back from the noise of the world in order to hear the purest and truest voice within. That meant long stretches of time without social media, television and social events. It was imperative that I put in the *10,000 hours* on mastering myself and becoming an expert at me. For years I was running myself ragged, burnt out for the sake of community service and calling it destiny. My life was imbalanced. I was going to be like all the freedom fighters that came before me, but I was doing it from a space of insecurity, trauma, pain and desperation. I struggled to place an emphasis on love, reflection, self care and grace. As I was encouraging everyone as a leader, friend and mate, I was hurting, depressed and struggling with loving myself. The things I gave to others, I failed to provide for myself. The lack of self care was my weakness. The lack of self care was my failure. I put so much pressure on myself that I broke myself. Was this necessary? Yes, because I surely wouldn't be where I am now if I had not.

There are some great mistakes that have provided some great lessons, from when I did not focus on me. Wisdom hurts sometimes. In turn my failures were indeed collateral damage for others, and for that I will always use my mistakes as stepping stones to a greater version of myself. The best apology you can provide in certain situations is bettering yourself. For that I am forever gracious. I am indeed wiser now. I feel older and sage-like. I randomly speak in parables. My students laugh and bring awareness to my grey hairs. They ask me for advice and say thank you for being you. I say it in return, honoring the gratuitous privilege that it is to be wise. To be an educator and role model. For that I am forever gracious, blessed, and highly favored!

"Life is a story; we are all building from the author within."
- @GregCorbinSpeaks

For years as activists we run around putting fires out, but often we fail at preserving ourselves. We never get to the root of an issue. Our fire is a flickering flame aiming to burn the walls of oppression, without burning ourselves. But we sometimes end up exhausted. When they can't use you anymore, they will toss you to the side and if you do not move out the way quick enough, they will blame you for their life challenges. Sometimes people place their cross to bare on your back, because they are afraid that they are not capable of carrying it on their own, and instead of asking for help in healthy ways, they will scapegoat you for their personal issues that they haven't confronted. Therefore it's not about you, it's about the them they are afraid to face.

Life is a story we are all building from the author within. I have played the guy who wanted to put out all the fires, operating from desperation and insecurity. Eventually the fires put me out. I am not alone. This is me embracing the Phoenix. The resurrection. I've operated from a source of pain and personal trauma and it was used to create real impact. I wonder what I can create operating from a space of self love, wholeness, and reflection.

EMBRACE YOUR PHOENIX

@GregCorbinSpeaks
(BUY THE T-SHIRT)

Worthy

Circle got smaller, everybody can't go - Nipsey Hussle

This morning I realized I was unsettled. I was missing something. I felt empty. I was unsure and insecure, rejecting the person I was, falling into the fear that I'm not valuable or good enough. I began drowning in the emotions of neglect and abandonment, swimming in slumped back pity, a signature for shame. Then I realized I was doing this to myself. I'm the root of my own neglect and rejection, which feeds my negative self image and self esteem. This is one of many moments I have to talk myself into the day with affirmation and admiration for how far I've come and how far I've got to go. There is so much in front of me that it overwhelms me. I haven't gotten centered in the last week or so. Not sure of the impetus, but I'm realizing there is some fear there, that I need to shake. But how?

The only person that can discover the source of this spirit is me. It's an internal battle.

I've got this.
I've got this.
I've got this.
- @GregCorbinSpeaks

I'm holding onto shame of my past mistakes and failures and bringing them into the present. Being hard on myself will not help. I must choose...

GRACE and **PATIENCE**

KINDNESS and PEACE

I am not my past.

My past informs who I am, and provides wisdom, so that I can move forward productively.

I will not allow my wounds to dictate my life. I will ambitiously and assertively examine and explore those wounds. I will transform the wound(s) into productive behaviors and impact. Hurt people hurt people, when they behave from a wounded place. I will not allow this wound to defeat me. I will learn my lesson and move towards glory.

I will not use my ability to practice low self esteem to reaffirm my addiction to suffering. I will not use past relationships where there was genuine love to reaffirm my addiction to emotions and hurt around betrayal.

I am more than my past. I will not allow my wounds to dictate my outcome. Those who are no longer in my life are not needed in my life. It is not a matter of deserving or an expression of privilege but a universal law that our relationship needs to practice something else. Although my carnal desires and emotions will try to conquer me, they will not win by preoccupying my thought process or soul energy.

This is what letting go is.
- @GregCorbinSpeaks

It is a process and like all processes there are many steps that need to take place. No, I am not fully free of my past wounds, chemical reactions, negative emotions, and thoughts. My personal reality is controlled by my perspective and the environment I create. .

Truth is, I miss the old friends that I can no longer talk to,

because the relationship ran its course.
The universe needs us to be something else for the world.
I miss them, but what is becoming clear is
I miss the old me that attracted those people into my life.
I am grieving, mourning moments when it was all good.
The sadness is exiting my heart and leaving behind
footprints of wisdom
from a well traveled road.
I invite the new friends, the new moments, as I change my heart
into a door that everyone else can't travel through,
because it is my door,
perfectly designed for me.

For all we know, we choose the plight, the painful and compelling argument that we are flesh filled robots internalizing a reality that lacks tangible authenticity. And it's become increasingly more difficult to spread the liberation.

Spiritual Healing Questions To Consider

The business plan attached to pain, trauma, suffering is a **DEEP WINDing HOLE** that is difficult to ignore once you identify how much $$$$$ is attached to hurt. Remember hurt people hurt people, broken people break people.

How much $$$$ is attached to the prison industry, pharmaceutical industry, medical industry, and education industry?

How many **JOBS** are necessary to sustain a collection of industries that is connected to the flow of information and the cycle of trauma?

How many **PEOPLE** are intertwined in services where healing is their main need?

And if the issues are actually fixed, will **HEALING** erase the problems that become wounds inside of the people servicing as micro-expressions of a bigger macro?

Will the **PROFIT** of business sectors be threatened if more healing occurs and will those jobs be secure if the hurt is not as present as it once was?

The Trap

The Trap, Music, Violence and The Moving Museum

*Trap: A subgenre of hip-hop that gets its name from the Atlanta slang word "**trap**", which refers to a place in which drugs are sold illegally.*

A prayer shout to call on ancestors, tongues holding a conversation with the divine, please provide light, the darkness is a mute nothing, pour the resurrection, slow, wine the hips until we are drunk on reproduction, but what are we creating in this cipher of exchange, where art is monopolized by consumerism, status chasing junkies struggling to discover meaning on their own, so they purchase the purpose of others until they feel like they know them personally, don't say that word, it doesn't belong to you, this is our rebirth of cool, arctic pen strokes, icicle quotes, numb eardrums..

When the body becomes a museum. Organs will become a sponge absorbing water, draining the surroundings. Downloading experiences, each story is an artifact sitting on display, activated by personal storylines creatively expressed. Manufactured by people who purchase tickets to the exhibit. There is always a performance to witness.

When the body becomes a museum, moving exhibits showcase stories as an extension of experience. Each song is a token of creative expression created by urban journalists sharing experiences that White or upper class folk can afford to visit via concert, but will most likely never visit in person because it's too dangerous. The artist embodies the experience and puts it on display for 90-120 mins per performance with lighting, sound, sonic ritual, vibrational magic that enters (entertainment = to enter and detain; hold captive) the body or bodies of water (simatics). Internalize the mood and tone and manifest the energy the sound waves carry. Music is manifestation.

There is an embedded history of violence in the country of America. It is so deeply woven in the DNA, that on some level many have internalized the yearning to witness conflict or cause drama. We've focused on trauma informed practices without a healing centered strategy for so long, we may have left the most digitally exposed generation without solutions to cope with information received. Did we diminish their ability to be resilient? Yes, we've collectively gained awareness, but we've positioned some youth and adults with no true outlet other than social media. In a digital culture it's easy to repress things when they may be healthier verbally communicated. Our teenagers of today move through busy worlds anxiously, addicted to their phones, struggling to deal with silence. They are craving noise and creating inner dialogue in thought bubbles that are never made public.

"We've focused on trauma informed practices without a healing centered strategy for so long, we may have left the most digitally exposed generation without solutions to cope with information received. Did we diminish their ability to be resilient?" - @GregCorbinSpeaks

As a Black Man in leadership it is beyond challenging...

Leadership Trauma, Finding Home

What happens when your 7 year old self shows up in the board meeting?

You know, those moments when you feel bullied, and the fear of imperfection and incompetence settles in like a fragile seashell on a sandy beach. One of the hardest things a person can experience is the sense of surveillance hovering over their every move. And one of the most difficult things to overcome is, the fear of failure that lives loudly in the confines of a mind.

As a leader, your people need you to be strong, resistant to openly discussing your insecurities, because there are moments when vulnerability works against you. Leadership is full of potholes pregnant with trap doors, welcoming your every move. As an executive I've experienced the need to be three times as good as my counterparts. When I missed an email exchange multiple times, it became part of an underground reputation. Yes it was true, I missed some emails. But I had to think about the privilege that was not afforded to myself, but was given to others with compassionate understanding.

Recently I went to an event that I've attended for years. It's a powerful networking event that can shift your net worth over time if you work the relationships correctly. The room is always festive with movers and shakers, people sending their best recreation, yet professional projections into reality. The body language of the event is constantly having a conversation ciphering around class dynamics mixed with race and politics, but all driven towards one key theme.

That is an opportunity.

My latest visit to this event was very interesting. I noticed something had changed, and nothing was the same. I spoke to multiple people who felt the same way. "It's not the same". The discovery that I had was powerful. I realized in that moment I was fully present, floating in an endless moment of the now.

They didn't feel the same, I didn't feel the same, because we weren't the same.

If we felt like we did five years ago that may be an indicator that we haven't grown in some ways. In that moment of now I noticed the performance that people have committed to, characters with descriptions expressing a script that they transmute consistently to reality. I thought to myself how addicted and dependent I used to be to public events.

Someone asked "Where have you been? Haven't seen you on social media or anything. Where ya been. I miss you."

I said in response "I've been inside. Just working on my home."

They said, "Oh that makes sense. You bought a house. I know how that can be. I own a few homes."

I responded and said, "No. I haven't bought a house yet. I'm inside of my home. I've been inside of myself studying my spirit, my emotional housing and the foundation, because home is where the heart is, so that's where I'm spending a lot of time."

I honestly thought they were going to walk away, because I wasn't interested in the performance. I was present with my truest now. They stayed and asked me questions about what I was doing differently. I shared my thoughts on stillness arts, like meditation and Qigong. We spoke for another 5 minutes celebrating the moment, settled in gratitude.

These events were playgrounds for me, moments of fun, spending the currency of time, paying with my attention in an economy of approval. Searching for validation, aiming to fill voids that I didn't have full comprehension that were even there. I noticed that I didn't always have relationships with people, but that people were often my addiction, because those interactions were attached to internal chemical reactions. So in hindsight I didn't have relationships, I had addictions. Some of those interactions were based on memorized emotions attached to an internal history of events that I was not fully aware of. Now I'm in a different space of thought, a shifting internal climate that is impacting the way I see my external reality, flipping a script that was performing a character that others approved of. And if others approved of the displayed performance, I received hits of dopamine with people pushing my like buttons. If you notice Facebook doesn't have a dislike button. There's a reason for that. One I won't explore at this current moment. Just check out the new Netflix documentary Social Dilemma.

People are craving something different these days. You can feel the vibration. People are yearning for something real and authentic, but it's challenging when authenticity is for sale.

Who are you without the realities the world has provided you? What are you without your core beliefs? What would you do differently if you no longer subscribed to any of the identities people use to classify and categorize you for their own needs of functionality?

Receiving revelations that there were moments where I didn't have relationships in my life, but I had addictions was more than just deep. Yes, in the context of relationships we related, but what is it that we found relative? I thought about my ex-girlfriends and how we served each other's craving for drama, subconsciously reproducing the experiences we had before meeting, conjuring self fulfilling prophecies that live deep in our core beliefs. That moment when we feel like we aren't good enough, because someone closed the door in our face at a birthday party when we were 7. Or that story you've used to boost sympathy when someone pushed you down some school steps during a snowstorm at the age of 10. Stories. We all have them. When we peel back the layers of our scripts, we can see the storylines exactly for what they are and how they were built. We become the stories we consistently feed ourselves. Retraining the wiring of the brain is challenging, because our cognitive reasoning is connected to our personality which is the mix of how a person shows up to reality.

It ain't the same.

It's not supposed to be the same, because you're not the same. You came here searching for a moment you enjoyed. A moment you were once in love with. And now that moment can no longer be found in this environment because you're no longer the same person you once were. Many people come to events searching for their past forgetting that the past is the past. We all have done it, expecting to get that feeling and emotional response that will provide the chemical reactions we've grown addicted to. So in reality, at times we don't have relationships. We have addictions. What do you mean?

You came here trying to rekindle a feeling of good times, but in real time that moment is one that is gone. It is a moment that you will never receive again. All you have is now. You're not who you were 5 years ago. Therefore your perspective has evolved and shifted. The search is the pursuit of happiness and not eternal joy. That is the addiction! Trying to build happiness out of external events, instead of investing inside of yourself.

"That's some real shit, G! It actually makes sense."

The question is what did this event provide for you before, that it can no longer provide for you in the now? And why is that? What void did it fill within you? And how did your spirit lead you back to this moment to have this conversation? What is it that your true self needs and is searching for? This event and other things are no longer doing that. Therefore you may need to sit still, go inside, and visit your home for a while. I know you may feel you're going to miss out by stepping back, what are you missing? A disappointing moment where your expectations fall short. I mean look! We are standing in a large ballroom watching the performers perform, acting out their scripts given to them through inheritance and socialization. We perform too. We're just lucky enough to be aware of the show and the roles we play.

Once you see with new eyes, you will see differently. You were seeing with a different pair of eyes 5 years ago. Your eyes have evolved and with your level of awareness has shifted your perspective. Once you see with new eyes, there is no unseeing. You have the power of choice and you can choose the lie of unseeing, but your awareness will always remind you of what you've seen. Once you notice, there will be more noticing to further amplify your growth and perspective. Your life will be less built around the options of a manufactured reality and more around an honest perspective of truth through your eyes. They are your eyes, your insight, your vision of reality. This is your dream that you make believe to be real. Therefore you make it real.

Heavy Shoulders

In the past I've allowed the people pleasing tendencies to get the best of me. Our wounds will decorate our decisions, especially in the roles of leadership. There is a parallel process that occurs when in these life positions. The energy we manifest will eventually mirror as outcomes through others in our lives, but only when we are observing life with a reflective and more mature eye. When operating from brokenness we move from a space of fear, lacking the confidence to make clear decisions that celebrate love. We act from a space of scarcity, fearing we don't have enough, leaving us with the feelings of being invaluable and worthless.

(Trap) I recall my aunt stating "nothing changed the way a person thinks like a television. When that TV, the boob tube was invented. It changed the world, because it tells you what to think, versus the radio which leaves room for interpretation and imagination. The first television was introduced to the world at the 1939 World Fair in New York City. Over the next decade, electrical innovators would make strides creating a more portable feature that would be able to sit in living rooms across the country.

Sometimes at work I feel insecure, like I'm hiding something. Like I don't know what I'm doing, and that generates a ball of confusion within that leads to instability internally and externally, which shows up in my management style. On one hand I realize the privilege and blessing it is to work in a mirroring position where I can see the reflection of it. In some way these last two days I've been wrestling with my level of competence. I feel insecure, confused, incapable and embarrassed. I'm not sure if I feel ashamed, but my fellow has let me know her concerns. In some ways she feels detached and segmented from the other working parts of the program. Old models of leadership were "stay in your place" models, where today's new structures challenge the old model, because it celebrates collaboration and togetherness. Not sure how my fellows trauma and home life experiences are playing out in this. Her father was abusive to the mother and the mother and her. She's still seeing what that has done to her. She's extremely self aware, and in many ways yearns to be involved, engaged on all fronts. My challenge as a leader is identifying what to share in order to invite her to see for the sake of her development.

Another challenge is my need to have things figured out or to always know what I'm doing. I need to be more disciplined with myself and at work in professional spaces. I need to get better with time. I also need to operate from the goal and not my world of ambition and imagination all the time. I haven't been grounded in the work and at points bored out of my mind. Wasting time and getting paid to just be. I'm not happy with that and I can't blame the fellow for how she is showing up, because in reality I created the environment and ecosystem for that reaction.

"Most leaders don't get to say they are afraid and definitely do not get to share the burden with others, therefore the concept of vulnerability does not always work in leadership." - @GregCorbinSpeaks

There is an overwhelming pressure whirling inside my chest, twisting tightly into my lungs. I'm anxious in the moment, running impatiently into the next moment, fearing that the present will birth another moment of failure. Yes this is anxiety, but this isn't about trauma more than it is about the lofty fear of success.

I've procrastinated at times, dancing between the lines of potential and promise. There are moments when I allow the burden to live heavy on my shoulders, until my shoulders grow tight with knots in my deltoids. I'm carrying my past into my future with this present moment. There are scientists who believe that we exist in different dimensions of ourselves simultaneously. Psychologists speak of the inner-child's ability to re engage it's older version of self in the adult form. But I keep going, running on fumes, aiming to complete my work plan. Never resting, because the idea of working on the weekend disrupts my self care, but not making this deadline sets me back. Decisions are knocking at my door. I choose to keep working. This isn't the healthiest choice, and knowing that I have "choice" is a powerful thing right now. I'm breathing bricks, working my way through the walls that my respiratory system is building.

Most leaders don't get to say they are afraid and definitely do not get to share the burden with others, therefore the concept of vulnerability does not always work in leadership.

It's a stressful moment and there are no mentors available to support me. This is where the mistakes happen. Where living moment to moment is not enough, because visionaries are always held hostage by the foreshadowing of a destiny that no one else is privy to. It's pressure. It's scary. It's a responsibility on steroids depending on how much you care about the futuristic illusion. Yes, I'm driving the ship and fighting hard not to sink it in an ocean of failure.

The decision is breathing down my back, and it's a must that I grab composure by its hand and walk it through the forest of my mind.

Visualization is where I travel.

There are leaders that operate from an old model that is celebrated by a perception of strength that highlights those who have the highest level of endurance. Was I doing this? Some are actually moving from fear, desperation, and scarcity. I was moving from fear. When fear triggers the emotional brain, it focuses on the threat at hand. But what do you do when the threat at hand is you?

When you become your own obstacle? The brain becomes trapped in a feedback loop of worry in which it rehearses all the things that can go wrong. Instead of visualizing success and prosperity, you become anchored in disappointment from an event that hasn't even occurred yet. This worry becomes an addiction for recovering people pleasers like myself, who've in the past internalized staff issues and allowed outside emotions and fears to dictate the decision making process.

"Carrying the burden alone is a choice and I am making better choices. I pray that you will as well." - @GregCorbinSpeaks

As a leader it's challenging to know when to say no and when to say yes. This is why strategy, goals and best practices are important. In moments of stress, where the clouds of decision making hover, your goals can serve as parameters that help you say no or yes with clarity. I am learning to delegate all things except my self confidence and faith. The heavy will turn light. Carrying the burden alone is a choice and I am making better choices. I pray that you will as well.

Questions on the Trap

What does it look like to hold someone personally responsible ?

Think deeply, what does the system's version of personal responsibility look like?

And how do we internalize that behavior and mechanism, so that we mimic it in some way?

How is racism built and manifested?

How is classism created and manifested?

How is islamophobia, homophobia, transphobia constructed, manifested and played out through human beings?

What is the common thread they all have in common ?

Is oppression deep rooted in the human experience, so deeply embedded in the fabric of everyday interactions and human conditioning that it is difficult to unwire the mental machinery of those behaviors?

Will people spend their entire lives fighting for a cause that may never fully manifest? And if this is the case will there always conflict, especially with social justice? How much money is made because of conflict and who is benefitting?

What happens to the human body and mind when it believes it always in a fight?

And if there is this ability to mimic systems are we building traps, as we build liberation from said system?

If we are incubated in the system, created by the system, don't we all have opportunities to be of the system until enlightened by others?

And if that enlightenment comes will it be shared with a loving vigor filled with compassion or will it be disproportionate and projected anger and rage from those who are in positions or moments of oppression?

Anger is justifiable and needs an outlet, but anger also doesn't provoke empathy and unfortunately it provokes an excuse for others to be ignored based on one's conditioning?

Are they socially engineered and built by ideologies, philosophies, and pedagogies that have been socially engineered by another engine called media or the source of informing those??

What is the point of playing this game when you begin to see it from every side, especially the one that is built in objectivity?

A side where you step back and use empathy to build a better understanding of the problem, so you can get to a solution?

PROTECT YOUR MIND.

PROTECT YOUR HEART.

@GregCorbinSpeaks

(BUY THE T-SHIRT)

The Body

Memo For Billie (This Body)

As an artist I learned early on from trainers, coaches and directors that the human body is a vessel for expression, and that one of the best things the body can experience is being hollow. Being an empty body allows energy to flow through you.

No one knows sacrifice like you Billie.

What made you sing *Strange Fruit*?

A song written by another person.
A song dedicated to lynched bodies.
Bodies that swing in the southern wind.

Bodies.....

This body   be benevolent beauty
                  be buried underneath it's underneath
                  be bone marrow sorrow serenity
                  be desensitized symphony
                  be suppressed oppression orchestra
                  be miraculous metaphor for open wound
                  be deeply memorized maps of pain trapped
                  be saltwater veins

This body   be home
                  be magic
                  be sanctuary and sin
                  be wizard and warlock
                  be weather vane and compass
                  be lighting and thunder

This body   be sun
                  be light

be shine
be shadow
be fire and brimstone

This body   be muse
be museum
be the museum
be on full display
be tokenized and commodified
be business plan and business model

This body   be scarred
be the healing
be the healed

This body   be past
be present
be future
be timeless.

(My Teenage) Body

It's 9th grade and everyone is having sex! I'm afraid of the v-word. Ok, I'll say it. Vagina. There I said it, vagina. Well, I'm not afraid of vagina. I'm afraid of my body. I'm afraid that my body parts will not be good enough for someone else's approval. Ok, hell with it! I was afraid my penis wasn't big enough to satisfy a female. I believe it was the small private parts jokes that I overheard during hallway transitions to class. Or maybe it was the stand up comics on Def Comedy Jam that created this internal terrorism around my self esteem.

And people wonder why the pre-teen-puberty-infested-youth run towards porn. It's the way you sneak to watch it, fast forwarding to your favorite fetish or curve to satisfy that media programmed bias implanted in your head from pop culture.

I would say I used my pursuit of porn as a way to compensate for the sexual experiences that I was missing out on, while my peers were indulging. And yes I lied on my penis. Courage was not my forte during those conversations where teenage boys gathered to brag about their conquest. The fear of being isolated and disbanded from certain circles motivated me to overcompensate.

What a belief?
The limited thought that having sex makes you cool.

It's a belief that you are only as good as your physical stature and what the body can perform. After a while I realized having sex didn't make you cool. I realized that effective communication, listening with patience long enough to figure out if the people I dated had something in common with me. Over time I learned a new cool that didn't center on sex. And that was cool enough for me.

Her Body

The pursuit of the body in the American context of discussion based deeply in colonialist principles of territorial gain and objectification.

We were taught, conditioned and trained to see the woman's body as something to own, so deeply ingrained was the resentment for being positioned in a body that was always devalued and systemically disadvantaged.

We barely wanted the body we were given due to the circumstances of oppressive conditions, so we compensated with the ability to control our lustful adventure to occupy the body of a woman.

To spend a night inside of a woman was the most celebrated victory my pubescent friends would discuss. We somehow attached this to manhood and masculinity, because it was what we knew. I remember one day walking down the street, seeing this sister with thick thighs, round hips and a nice sized buttocks. When I saw her face I was immediately turned down, but not all the way off. There was still a curiosity lingering. And then she smiled.

With previous encounters, I've had moments when I was no longer interested. So I had to ask myself this deep burning question, "Where does this thought come from?"

Yeah, that was fun. Unlearning. I was operating from a space of incessant ignorance.

My Body: On Marriage

"We forgot to tell Greg that he didn't just gain a wife, but he also just gained an extra 20 pounds.

It's called marriage weight.

He should also be ready to buy some new clothes because he won't be able to fit the ones he has now."

- Two of my dear friends.

Battling Weight

My entire life I've battled weight, carried it as if the only way to breath was by holding onto things outside of me. The fear of letting go is a selfish energy in some ways. I recall becoming consumed with the thoughts from the mouths of others. Being concerned about what others thought about me triggered some behaviors that were once rooted in the core of my being.

Like many, as a child I didn't receive enough positive attention because of the way I dressed, because I was the nerd in class and because of the weight I carried. As I've grown and evolved through life, I've learned to see the painful events differently. I've learned to visually stage the event outside of me as a moment in time, platformed in a different era of my life. This has empowered me to not only acknowledge that it happened, but to explore, investigate how I played a role in manufacturing and manifesting the outcome.

When I see it as a past event, I strengthen my ability to be accountable and responsible for my future, because the lessons not only live forever in my cellular memory and subconscious mind, but will possibly present themselves again to test my wisdom and promote me to another level of mastery. This is the school of life, constantly placing human beings in classrooms where learning opportunities have potential to become teachable moments for others if we learn the lesson properly and efficiently. Those teachable moments become an etched lesson plan staged as a living document in the soul, but only if you're willing to work hard by incorporating the practice of introspection through stillness arts such as meditation, yoga, qi gong, etc.

My entire life I've battled weight.

And you may be asking yourself, why does he repeat this line? And this was not too long ago,,,

My entire life I've battled weight.

There were moments in my life where I made decisions to be the caretakers of others, when I should have made different choices that would have prevented this. I was unaware of personal boundaries, never really considering the time spent trying to make others feel better about the hard lessons' life was delivering. I never noticed how much I was interfering with the learning curves of others.

Sometimes we frame our efforts to assist others as saving instead of providing help or support. I was blocking the lessons for people to learn on their own and do their personal work. I was not only blocking their lessons, but their blessings as well. It was never my work to do, but working the work of others became a high for me, a source of validation, where I looked forward to helping the broken birds as my aunt would say. Eventually seeing others fly higher grew to become more important than seeing myself fly higher, because the high of witnessing someone's ability to take flight became a reflection of my personal potential and self-esteem. Let me be clear, there is nothing wrong with helping others, but we have to think about our personal intentions. Is the help for them or is it for you? Yes, it feels good to help other human beings, but is the "feeling good" about you or them? I say that because sometimes the work will not feel good, and if it's about feeling good then the work will not last. Some people stop working on themselves because they understand how much work really goes into transformation. It is a hard and difficult thing.

My entire life I've battled weight.

Now yes, I got a lot of work completed through helping others, but the platform of reflection empowers me to see it from a different angle. That is wisdom working in my highest favor, because I am not emotionally attached to the memory, but I am more interested in the wisdom gained, and how it can help others receive their lessons sooner. The difference now is I realize that if a person is not interested in doing their own work, they may not be open to learning how to do their own work. You can't coach the uncoachable, but you can leave them to their own devices and watch the show play out. That will prevent you from overstepping your boundaries to carry the workload, absolving you from responsibility for their failures, because you are no longer investing your energy into their outcomes. This gives them an opportunity to look at themselves without the distractions of others, because you've realized that your support, although you mean well is enabling them and draining you. This is mainly because the balance of obligation is off. You are only obligated to carry your work, not the work of others. Say no with kind conviction, and gracefully move through life.

My entire life I've battled weight.

I enjoy riding my bike to work. It gets my legs working, my mind working, and my ears working. I listen to my inner thoughts deeply working towards awareness and full connection. I also enjoy saving money on Uber. That's work as well. While riding to work one day in 23-degree weather I had an ice chilled thought melt into a puddle of wisdom. I realized I walked into a fast-paced environment that celebrated its scrappy and aggressive identity, and while celebrating that persona the organization neglected the needs of the people living inside of its body.

It's interesting how organs have the ability to turn on one another, and how the body is designed to get rid of any foreign visitors that work against its core values and will to survive. Those core values help manifest a culture that can only change from the inside out.

Black Body

Another moment of silence.
Another piece of history.
Another brown face.
Another brown body.

Another moment where we all try to unravel the systemic danger
of being Black in America.

Another chance for trending topics and hyperbolic conversation
that is commodified into a pocket of entertainment.

Another unjust use of power.
Another media pull on the obvious.

Another opportunity
                to transform something ugly like
                abuse of power
                into power for the abused.

Another moment to build momentum.

Another walk of faith
                where we are distracted by holidays
                and the check to check grind
                that has us chasing the tail of the
                American Dream.

Another timeline full of talk
                too much damn talk
                and not enough innovation and creativity.

Another pile up of CNN debates and media propaganda .

Another moment where the media controls
                the emotional capacity of the people.

Another...

#RIP To every Black Body that has fallen.

State Property

2 for 5
2 for 5
Ooop ooo
2 for 5
2 for 5
Ooop ooo
We understand in the back of your mind
You're trying to survive and stay alive
But while you're yelling "2 for 5"
Congress yellin' "5-10"
Senate yellin' "5-10"
Government yellin' "5-10"
Give them black men 5-10
75% of the prison population is black men
Your skin, is worth millions
Ask Michael Vick
Ask Michael Tyson
Ask Michael Jordan
Ask Michael Jackson
He hustles in the white tee
On the block in his white tee
Got locked up in his white
Let him go in his white tee
Back to block in his white tee
Got shot in his white
Died in his white tee
Probably gonna bury him...in his white tee
And that's how the story be
He dropped out outrageously
In the 8th grade graciously
Accepting the application to the streets of hard knocks
But
No one can hear the knocks of opportunity when your door's locked

And inside your house of opportunity is hard crack rocks and boiling pots
That boil hot like Sodom's lots
And since repetition is nothing new
Most humans don't mind being robots
Third eyes, minds, blind to the plot
That slavery never stopped
that 's why the cop's cock loaded 9 millimeters
Make you run 90 meters
How the police gonna be my brother's keeper when they blowing out our backs like speakers
All that's left is the blood on the sneakers
And the funerals aren't getting any cheaper
That's why the busiest speaker in the community is the preacher
Because the bullets have no names written on them
Is it really worth standing on that corner
Risking the automatic jail time
Your life should've come with a for sale sign
Because when the bail does not show up on time
This wicked system doesn't mind reducing you to a couple of numbers and some dollar signs
It's just monetary gain or monetary gain for the stress and the strain
Your life is nothing but another worthless blood stain
Your freedom had been stolen
Labeled state property
Just another novelty
A ward of the state
Controlled by wardens of the state
And this beautiful government structure does not mind treating young black bodies like prime real estate
So, two cellmates, that's a duplex
Three cellmates, that's a triplex
Four cellmates, that's an apartment complex
All one big prison complex
Situation's not that complex
When they'll build prisons more than schools

Condominiums more than schools
Casinos more than schools
And we play the fool
As the crime rates increase and the death rates do too
Understand this, My people, my beautiful people
You get a felony on your record it's hard for you to become a
cashier at Rite Aid
Or ring up a check burger at checkers
It's just that hard to get a job
Cuz' who wants to trust an ex-convict
And who wants to love an ex-convict
And we stand here as the real convicts
Victims of the 13th Amendment
So while you're yellin'
2 for 5
2 for 5
Ooop ooo
2 for 5
2 for 5
Ooop ooo
We understand in the back of your mind
You're trying to survive and stay alive
But while you're yelling "2 for 5"
Congress yellin' "5-10"
Senate yellin' "5-10"
Government yellin' "5-10"
Give them black men 5-10
75% of the prison population is black men
Your skin, is worth millions
Ask Michael Vick
Ask Michael Tyson
Ask Michael Jordan
Ask Michael Jackson
Ask Barack Obama
Ask
Their mamas
When they lock up these blacks men

They are locking up our future fathers
If they keep locking up all the fathers
There may not be enough fathers to father the sons
They are banking on your billion dollar bad decision making
To feed the rural communities
Because there is no more coal to dig
No more oil to frack
Its a pipeline of chaos and the war of drugs
To the terminology of the super predator
Its all a plan supply and demand
We got melanin for sale
There's melanin for sale
There's melanin for sale
Your skin is worth millions
Your skin is worth millions
Your skin is worth millions

So,
Whose property are you?

(Take Care of Your) Body

My father passed away from lung cancer when he was 49, just like Stuart Scott.

My late friend MJ Harris passed away from cancer at just 30 years old.

If you think your career is more important than your body which makes your purpose possible please re arrange your thinking on this issue. We have to take care of our bodies, minds, spirits! We have too. No more of the mentality, "you have to die some day and some way." That is not our best. That is ambitious, powerless and limited thinking. We have too much divinity for that way of speaking. We have to teach this newer generation newer ways of healthy living. We must find a way to make it cool. Diabetes, arthritis, cancer, strokes and so much more happen because of how we treat our bodies and what we are trained to put in them. There's room to do better. It's never too late. Old and young. Never.

(Her Mind and) Body: Breathe

She looks incredible
Damn right unforgettable
Just unbelievable
Ask her what's going on inside of her eyes
What you wanna be when you grow up?
She tells me
I wanna be like Beyonce, Ciara and Rihanna
And it doesn't surprise me
Due to the blond weave
And the light-skin complexion
And the imagery on BET
And the fact that they all look the same
And she just had a baby 2 months ago
And she wishes it was so simple
Stretch marks of depression mark her self-esteem
Once a beauty queen
Relying on maybelline
A well-oiled machine
She wears tight jeans and see-through shirts
to boost her
self-esteem
Gain attention from wandering eyes
Using her thighs to gain acceptance
Like it's cool to be addicted to erections
And not to mention
She's no longer using protection
She is a falling star in a universe of low expectations
Wanting to be dead before the age of 18
Hoping death is the answer to all things
And all her frustrations
She is made more miseducation
200 years of Willie Lynch
A single-parent home
A psychiatrist that prescribes Ridilin

because her mother
has a drug addiction
200 years of self-hatred
Throwing on weaves and makeup
She looks 40 in the face
The breast
The waist
But she's really 15
Rocking contacts that's green
In a see-through shirt and tight tight jeans
Vividly wearing her self-esteem on her sleeve
And she can't wait for Christmas Eve
So she can receive
The finer things in life
Like the new trends in fashion
She ain't gotta open her mouth
Her physical do the braggin'
You know
The way she walks
The way she talks
She can walk by a group of guys with no applause
While she walking in passion pink pumps
Cause she look
5'11" in heels
But she really 5'7" for real
Selling nickel bags of weed for her uncle
To pay her cell phone bill
Body is like 30
But the mind is like 9
Soul is dirty so becoming spiritual
is damn near impossible
But her mother's in front of a corner store
Acting like a well-known hoar
Father's caught inside of a jail cell
Trying to rearrange his religion
Trying to find Jesus in between the lines of the Quran
He's searching for a reason

Searching for a meaning
But only God can stop the bleeding
So
What do you tell the future when they do not know their past?
They're running like presents with cold hard cash
Are they really worth the Malcom X ...(??)
Or what if MLKing saw all the oil spills
So what do you tell the future?
Tell her that she is loved
She is strength
She is power
Ambition
She is Harriet Tubman
In the flesh
Mary Mcleod Bethune in the flesh
Coretta Scott King in the flesh
Birthing nations of a
Martin Luther King
Of a
Malcolm X
A Marcus Garvey
She is not lil' Kim
Or Foxy Brown
Or Jackie O
Or Trina
Or could any of us afford another video ho ridin' around
Because she's got so much to live for
So next time you see her
Walking down the street
Don't judge her
Just love her
Whether she be a queen or promiscuous
And tell her
She is now free   free   free   free

See Through Body: Invisible Man

For Michael Vick and all the black athletes who have felt this way.

You run so fast. You run so quick, so elusive,
    because you are afraid to be vulnerable,
    afraid to be touched
    to be Dialo
    to be Patrice
    to be Coltrane
    to be Martin
    to be Malcolm
    to be Ellison.
    because you are invisible man

There is no wearing your heart on your sleeve.
Your skillset is breathtaking.
Your speed snatches the lungs of my eyesight of amazement.

I stare at idiotic boxes
on Sunday afternoon
watching you jump over defenders
    never forgetting how invisible black men used to be.
    how those magical legs would have one day
    had you running from plantation owners
    who used to trade you for sheep, for cattle, for three-fifths,
    for profit, for business, for houses
    for livestock, for livestock
    yes you were livestock.

Especially when you're sweating' on that field,
    that broken field of dreams.
    They call you a quarterback,
    because you are not even a whole person.

There was a time when too much exposure
  would have gotten your neck
  snapped, chopped and screwed

Truth is some people care about their pets than people
  more about their dogs more than people
  more about the bark and the sound of their being
  than the words of your freedom.

They say you trained them how to fight til' the death
  to be vicious and loyal,
  as if they were house negros
  and then you water-hosed them
  as if they were marching for freedom
  only to hang them out to dry
  as their bodies squirmed like strange fruit.

  I guess you were barking up the wrong tree

But we understand you are just acting out your reflection
  this country of contradictions.

Funny how the same dogs that once hunted
  chased and killed slaves now have more rights
  than the humans who were slaves in the first place.

So it's not surprising when your multi-million dollar contracts
  become slave papers
  and the fans
  want to hang you out to dry
  for calling the wrong play
  with your pigskin skin
  a tangent for darkness
  a tar baby with a shotgun for an arm
  locked and loaded
  throwing bullets of blasphemy for yardage
  what is a man to do

when the speed of his legs
is more important than the intellect of his brain
when he is treated like product
a piece of meat
be-headed for stardom
running on chalk lines in the burning blazing sunshine
because ain't no time like gametime
no one can throw a ball like a mandingo do

It's in your bloodstream
don't you get it
don't you see it
don't your opponents look like a forest
do you remember Harriet Tubman with a shotgun for an arm
don't your owner in the skybox
playing god
look like your great great great grandmothers rapist
don't you see it
        it's gametime

        It's Emmitt Till in shoulder pads
        It's Medgar Evers in cleats
        It's Joe Lewis without a uniform
        It's Sean Bell
            Mike Brown
            Tamir Rice
             without their helmets

It's an illusion
a disappearing act
smoke and mirrors
a cloudy reflection
of how you used to show that coffin shaped smile
with tombstone teeth
how many muscles does a man use
when it comes to selling his body and soul
but we understand that you are afraid

to be touched
to be vulnerable
to have feeling

So go deep
      go deep
      go deep   go deep
                go deep
                and catch the breath of life
                before they hang you out to dry
                like the dog they proclaimed you are
      because
      you are not
      an animal
      a monster
      or a beast

You are human
You are human
You are human
You are such a beautiful human being.

PROTECT YOUR ENERGY. PROTECT YOUR PEACE.

@GregCorbinSpeaks

(BUY THE T-SHIRT)

Fictional Non-Fiction

An Interview For Jessica Rabbit

In one of my favorite movies, Jessica Rabbit danced in front of my eight year old eyes. In Who Framed Roger Rabbit an animated character seduced a human one. She had the curves of Beyoncé and my full attention.

Only after I stopped thinking with my head down there, did I even consider with my head up here, these questions about Jessica Rabbit:

1. How does the OBJECTIFICATION of an actual person compare and contrast to the objectification of an animated character?

2. Who was Roger Rabbit? Who is Jessica Rabbit? Who really got framed in the movie and How did their portrayals affect children in 1988 when it was released?

3. How does the brain process sexualized imagery at 7-10 years of age?

4. What was the socio/politcal environment regarding sex like when you took the trip to the movies?

5. What images reinforced the stereotypes later on in your teenage years and what is happening cognitively at that point in life?

6. How can we bring wholeness to this dialogue? And how do we heal the narratives of objectifying women? What does the unlearning look like?

Own Your Sh*t

Everything that irritates us about others can lead us to an understanding of ourselves. - Carl Jung [1]

What does it mean to be accountable? To be responsible for your actions. It means to take ownership of your behaviors, attitudes and thoughts. Sometimes it is easy and other times it is not. What does it mean to own your sh*t? What does it mean to own the excellent excrement or the fantastic feces? You know, sh*t. You know the sh*t that convinces us that we have nothing to work on. You know the sh*t that tricks us into believing that we are perfect.

We all have some parts of us that are beautiful and some parts that are ugly.

The **shadow,** a term coined by psychologist Carl Jung features the things we don't want to admit to having. It exists as part of the unconscious mind and is composed of repressed ideas, weaknesses, desires, instincts, and shortcomings. The parts of our personality that we submerge. The tiny nuances of perceived ugly that we've been taught to hide deep in the abyss of self, tucked away in the trenches of our mind. These are the parts we think others will not be able to love us through, so we disown those parts.

Sometimes we allow our ego to block us from producing the humility to own our mistakes and missteps, because we want to be right. Trust I have been there. Defensive and protective. It's like holding down a fort in fear that someone is going to find out who you really are, which may lead to not being accepted. We have been conditioned to believe being wrong may mean we are imperfect, unworthy, and invaluable, when in reality that is far from the truth. Why?! Humans are imperfect, yet humans are worthy and valuable. Being wrong, that is the spell we must shake off to produce healthier relationships that can endure conflict and chaos.

Being wrong means we are human, and admitting it expands our possibility. That is the **light** at work.

"You have an opportunity to either embrace this part of you to reflect and connect or reject and disconnect."
- @GregCorbinSpeaks

The dark side of yourself is yearning for your light, but you have programmed your mind to turn away from it. It is calling for your recognition, a sense of acknowledgement, but you are neglecting it, therefore abandoning yourself. You have an opportunity to either embrace this part of you to reflect and connect or reject and disconnect. What would you choose? How will you choose? When we embrace the parts of ourselves that we have been conditioned to ignore, we learn how to love, forgive, and practice patience with a gentle approach that heightens our self esteem, authenticity and honors the entire human experience within. By doing this innerwork we are creating the ability to love others when we see the same behaviors, attitudes and thoughts manifest through them. We treat people how we treat ourselves. The more we pursue the inward, the closer we get to ourselves, and the closer we get to others.

"We all have bags that we carry and it takes courage to unpack them with radical intention." - @GregCorbinSpeaks

Compassion is the key that unlocks the potential needed to mend the spiritual brokenness that many of us experience during life. We all have bags that we carry and it takes courage to unpack them with radical intention. No matter how uncomfortable. Through awareness and attention to detail we create space for ownership of our full selves without the yearning to lease responsibility when convenient. We own everything that we produce, because we have the mature understanding that we are responsible for what we generate. For what we manifest in relationship with people, in relationship with the planet and in relationship with the systems humans have created and inherited. We have power in each dynamic and connection that we are blessed to experience.

So yeah, own your sh*t. Own your fantastic feces and excellent excrement. For it brings you balance, as well as opportunity for ever growing wisdom with infinite learning curves and openings to strengthen empathy. Practice reflection, create space for inner dialogue and provide yourself constructive feedback. It is the courage to lean on your tribe when you are not at your best. When you need to be reminded how bright you can shine. Life is a negotiation between your light and your shadow. The choice is yours.

"Until you make the unconscious conscious, it will direct your life and you will call it fate." - Carl Jung 2

Tupac's Escape Plan: An Ode to the Bishop of Juice

Sources close to Tupac remarked, in response to his demeanor post-dropbox, "After playing the role of Bishop in the 1992 urban smash hit [*Juice*], he was never the same." 3

Tupac was one of the most gifted artists of our time. He was deeply invested in the state of humanity, and particularly compassionate towards the unfortunate predicaments of marginalized people of color. He understood the psyche of the human condition so clearly that he created a powerful acronym, by which he lived his personal and professional life:

T.H.U.G.L.I.F.E (The Hate You Give Little Infants F*** Everyone). 4

In the early 90's many would see the emergence of a thought provoking, charismatic, talented hip hop artist, poet, background dancer, and actor named Tupac Shakur. With a deeply educated mind, trauma filled upbringing he spoke from an experience that many could find a connection with. There was no one like Tupac. The first song I heard from him was *Brenda's Got A Baby*, in which he delicately and methodically shares a story of a pre-teen pregnancy. The video debuted on BET in 1992 and is still a startling reminder of his abilities as an artist to convey such truth. It was Black and White. It was done in the urban area of a city, with Ethel Love as Brenda and directed by Allan Hughes.

The video was purposely organized in a way to give the viewer the grimy feel of a gutter laced area hit by socioeconomic challenges. I can easily say watching *Brenda's Got A Baby* was one of my first times experiencing an emotional contagion that art can bring to its audience. I felt Brenda's fear, not just lyrically, but visually. Tupac's rigorously detailed expression, created a storytelling experience that was hard to find in Hip Hop at the time. In other words "I felt that shit."

72

A flexible, risk taking thinker, boldly open minded, Tupac was lyrically direct with his ever stinging critique of politics and its impact on everyday people. He was a melanin filled container for the emotion of those abandoned by a social system, built on their backs, and with their hands. He carried the pity, repressed rage, jubilant joy of survival, curiosity of intelligence, mounted frustration, undying love, triumphant confidence of people who looked just like him. He was a full expression of the human complexities absorbed from his many walks of life. Internalizing the energy of Baltimore and Oakland, mixed with an Islamic background, while soaking in the ideology of Black Nationalism, Tupac was ever courageous to say what he felt with his full heart and soul. Even if some people didn't agree, he always seemed to be fully alive and immersed in what he spoke.

He embodied so much passion. Passion, derived from the Latin word *passio*, meaning suffering is a perfect word to describe this artist to the core. Tupac was relentless both in the studio and with a movie script. In some ways he seemed tormented from having a high level of intelligence, witnessing many social ills bring pain to his communities. He cared deeply for those left in un-nurtured and isolated due to the haunting systemic oppression of marginalized people from many walks. Some may say he had compassion fatigue and needed a constant cathartic release from carrying the full scope and comprehension of the people's pain. From top to bottom, he understood the impact of poverty, inequality and injustice. He was known to do 7 songs a day when he was in the midst of recording.

So in 1992 when Tupac Shakur played Bishop in the movie *Juice* he's at a pivotal and prolific point in his career.

As a high school teenager, Bishop falls in lust with the unrelenting power of a gun.

Unfortunately, after a botched robbery he kills someone. After police interrogate the friends over the incident Bishop still craves for the commitment of his friends, but nothing is the same. This leads Bishop into a dark space of grief and control seeking behaviors. Feeling betrayed by the severed friendships, he eventually spreads rumors about one of the crew members by pinning the murders on him, and plans to kill the friends. The movie ends with a tussle between former friend Q played by Omar Epps. Q in a last chance effort fails to save Bishop who falls to his death. Many believe that Tupac was never the same after absorbing and performing the role of Bishop. Although the character died in the movie, it's possible Tupac kept the character alive, never fully releasing the remnants of such a troubled person, which could have fragmented his psychological makeup. Bishop is known for the famous line in which he stands by a locker and says to Q, "You think I'm crazy. I am crazy and I don't give a fuck. I don't give a fuck about you. I don't even give fuck about my damn self."

With this groundbreaking role, Tupac developed a similar edge, internalizing the fears manifested from urban environments that leave young children in predicaments where neglect and needs not being met is second nature. We see the pattern of accountability seemingly always falling on those raised in problematic ecosystems that do not foster whole people, but thrive on the brokenness of those who internalize and cultivate negative behaviors as survival mechanisms and responses to being rendered disposed or invaluable.

We have been conditioned to place blame on the body performing the act and not the system. If cancer develops in a body from smoking do you blame the person or the cigarette? Do you blame the previous generations who knew not of its dangers or do you place blame on the stressors that need to be numbed by a habit or addiction of relief ? Do you place blame on those who make their money off of the cigarettes or do you blame people for not being strong enough to get rid of the habit? Most likely you place blame on the person inhaling 15 cigarettes a day, striving for relief, because unhealthy points of release and self care are celebrated in this country, which feeds on pain, suffering and brokenness.

We live in a country/society that is founded on snatching land from people and objectifying brown bodies for free labor. This country is founded on spiritual brokenness, cognitive dissonance, greed, and acts of immoral insanity that is rendered justified by History textbooks to upkeep a narrative of power. Bishop was looking for power. Tupac was looking for power. They are both searching for balance in a disharmonious society that continuously takes from their contributions, while constantly making them the enemy of state.

Additionally, the role of Bishop amplified the ever growing legend of Tupac. Sourced from a real place, he energetically carried the character with such electricity, ferocity, and pure intensity that it was hard to ignore the impact.

On April 11th, 1992 almost 4 months after *Juice* made its debut, while high on cocaine and cannabis, Ronald Ray Howard would shoot a Texas State Trooper in the neck after being pulled over for a broken headlight. He would later say he was conditioned by rap music to hate police. His lawyer would use this for defense and cite that Tupac's *Soulja Story* incited Ronald to kill. On September 22nd, 1992 Dan Quayle would make the statement, "2Pacalypse Now, has no place in our society."

When Quayle made that comment, what many heard was not only did Tupac's voice not matter, but anyone in bodies laced with melanin who had similar stories did not matter as well. It underscored a belief that these voices and experiences were not welcomed in the public eye and must remain trapped in impoverished and disenfranchised environments, silenced in their suffering. Tupac ambitiously seized his material from personal experiences, news stories, and witnessing other's experiences, therefore Quayle's words were a full out expression of cognitive dissonance connected to a political agenda deeply tied to controlling cultural exposure and impact. Especially when the vessels for these stories were encased in Black and Brown bodies.

Yes, there was a former Vice President that would say that aloud in a country built on violence and conflict. Tupac literally grabbed his material from his personal experiences, news stories, and witnessing others experiences. Ernest Dickerson's well-crafted Bishop wasn't a falsehood in society. It was a genuine and raw expression of the truth. It didn't just create a criminal, it humanized one, providing the looking glass for the audience to see how people are manufactured by their surroundings and levels of exposure.

One would argue that the former Republican Party VP was using 2Pac as an opportunity to build a political platform for his own run at the presidency. Another argument one could use is that he's right: Responses to systemic oppression that are cultivated by the lack of opportunity, lack of equity across the board do not belong in our society. Job creation, better schools, etc., belong in our society. Once again citing the symptom through the body of Black Men and not deeply engaging and exploring the symptoms in the ecosystem that create the response. Our argument is that Quayle is saying there is no room for your story in society, and your experience is the America we don't want to acknowledge, therefore we need to ignore you because you remind us of our own cognitive dissonance and conflicts between morality and responsibility.

Tupac was an artist searching for refuge in the chair of a therapist that he didn't know existed. It's challenging to identify a practice that isn't practiced in the community you reside in. If only mental health was an established practice in communities of color. Art is a needs assessment. And Tupac needed an escape plan. Tupac also needed a supportive inner circle and family that would hold him accountable to him being his best self. The best version of himself. He didn't have an escape plan and many people outside of art don't have one either.

Erik Killmonger

Years have passed since the success of the blockbuster *Black Panther* graced movie screens, leaving all its haters in the dust. It's legendary financial blitz at the box office had it grossing upwards of $1 billion dollars. The movie was a "stone in the ocean" of the African-American experience, hitting the social media waves with #wakanda forever and suggesting attendees dress their bodies in the finest of African-inspired garb. Hailed as a culture-shifting moment, many people of color were inspired to collectively explore the contents of freedom and oppression. Going to the movies that weekend was a burst of Black and African Pride! Dashikis, Kente Cloth, Mud Cloth, and so much more.

I remember reading that Michael B. Jordan's portrayal of villain/hero Erik *Killmonger* Stephens sent him to therapy. As a character in society, *Killmonger* was cultivated by a country walking in its own condemnation of this oppression.

So what created Killmonger, a human being, black man, cultivated by an impoverished community where crime and violence serve as symptoms to a bigger issue?

Was it the lack of resources, leading to fear and desperation rooted in the foundation of greed? Or a country brooding in its own scarcity consciousness, moving through the emotional contagion of its deeply embedded roots, manifesting as bared fruits of destruction? Men who've been designed by their surroundings to implode from constant intergenerational trauma and persecution.

Killmonger isn't born, he's created.

I've realized I was given the story, the narrative, and past sufferings of my elders and ancestors. I've absorbed the events of the past with my heart, mind and soul, only to ask why? Why am I carrying the burden of a past? In theory I know the answer. It's because I was born into a black body with black parents and now I am destined to carry that torch. It's like peer pressure. If you say anything remotely close to thoughtful or against the argument of pain and suffering, especially tied to slavery, then you're immediately labeled an outcast.

Let's step back for a second. An onscreen character that doesn't exist in reality, developed, crafted and internalized by the mind of a brilliant and talented actor caused him to seek therapy. Whoa. This speaks volumes about the roles we inherit in a capitalistic system influenced by the global impact of colonialism.

In an online article, Michael B. Jordan shared these thoughts, "I was by myself, isolating myself. I figured Erik, his childhood growing up was pretty lonely. He didn't have a lot of people he could talk to about this place called Wakanda that didn't exist."

After hearing that, I felt as if he was telling part of my story. As an actor myself, I've also played characters that were challenging to shake loose. I've caught myself walking and enunciating words just like the characters I've played. You can't help but take on the trauma, the joy, the conflict of the writer's creation. The development of a backstory for an actor runs that deep. Entering the mind of a scripted character like *Killmonger* is risky and it takes courage, focus and a steady precision to execute the full expression and experience.

So let's dig deeper into the construction of the character *of Killmonger*: A human being and black male growing up in Oakland, CA after discovering his father dead in the living room of his Queens-home, who is cultivated by an impoverished community where crime and violence serve as symptoms to a bigger issue; a considerable lack of resources, which leads to fear and desperation rooted in the foundation of greed.

Meanwhile, a country brooding in its own scarcity of consciousness, moves through the emotional contagion of its deeply embedded roots manifesting as the bared fruit of destruction.

Erik is of the lineage of those who've been designed by their surroundings to implode from intergenerational trauma and persecution.

Killmonger isn't born, but created. An invention of systematic disenfranchisement, injustice and inequality.

In today's society, it's easy to mislabel people as toxic without thinking of their background or backstory. We must remember people are products of their environment.

Although fictitious, *Killmonger* is a character that many people can relate to. His explosive anger is expressed through strategic planning in order to take a crown from those who forgot he existed. His pain was invoked from being disposed, rejected, and abandoned by his family, only to transform rage from the death of his father into a soldier mentality for those he knew to be the most vulnerable. *Killmonger* cites that the war taking place on the poor and disenfranchised is an imbalanced conflict in which the oppressor dominates the outcome, because they have not just the guns and ammunition, but also the systems that are built to protect an inferiority complex. Although this character lives on screen in a virtual reality, it is scripted to express the ever growing angst of 400 plus years of colonized people forced to build a country they still have not received reparations from.

We deny these many possibilities that are conjured from when people (real or fictitious) are products of their environment. A toxic environment can produce damaging results to the body and mind.

Inspired by Jordan Peele's "US"

On Reawakening the Inner Child.

Yes I went to see the movie. It is an amazing and insightful piece of artwork. Yes the movie does carry symbolism, social commentary around race and class. But I want to go a different route.There are many of **"US"** with inner children muted underneath the noise of the **"US."** As the **"US"** runs its machine full of structured chaos, we all find ways to adapt to many of its patterns. The socialized personas inherited and produced by our primary surroundings become engrained deeply. For some, homes that appear as shelled houses is the first experience in community. If lucky enough we may receive the opportunity to control our first domain, our bedrooms. It's the first time for **"US"** to practice a sense of ownership inside of the **"US."** When old enough we grow conscious that we do have some agency and autonomy, deciding where furniture, pictures, and clothing can be placed. It's an artistic expression where we learn to manipulate the physical dimensions of reality through spatial, tactile and visual learning skills. This helps "US" express our creativity.

There's something deeper happening in **"US."** There's a hunger within that is being ignored, growing lust filled in the pursuit of happiness, dwelling in ideological lifestyles of the rich and famous, Never having enough, or feeling valuable and worthy, because the constant comparison to everything else can breed depression. The deep sitting truths of **"US"** reveals that the sins of man; greed, envy, lust, neglect are consistently expressed through thrill seeking behaviors condensed in self destructive norms built around business plans and models for an addiction called capitalism. In many cases children are not set up to find their voice, because of the constant systems of inheritance that live in the practice of socialization. This is how the **"US"** builds **"US."**

I recall a moment years ago while I was teaching in a classroom. I realized that I wasn't facilitating a learning journey for the students, but rather projecting my desires and dictating their critical thinking by giving away answers based on my own personal belief system. I wasn't leading the students through an experiential lesson, but a lecture that left little room for challenge and questioning. I allowed my angst of the **"US"** and pressure of the **"US"** curriculum to dominate my pedagogical approach and practice in those moments. By not allowing critical thinking to fully manifest in the classroom, I also created an environment that simultaneously created the energy of oppression and a learning environment that didn't maximize or encourage the students' voice.

Why would I do that? Not just school pressure drenched in creativity stealing energy like standardized testing. But the adults around me beginning with my parents did it to me. They were literally passing down the things they internalized from the **"US"** and were giving away the contagious disease that the **"US"** carries into **"US."** It's what a therapist would call a parallel process. We externalize what we've internalized through our childhoods. I call this, "The Great Repression!"

"Due to the notorious and inhumane invention of slavery and racism by the "US," our elders and ancestors did many things from a space of fear and need to keep their children safe."
- @GregCorbinSpeaks

My parents grew up in an era and environment that did not honor the child's emotions and in turn did not always meet my emotional needs. They were doing what they were taught because their parents said to them "Do as I say. I don't want no talkback. No sass." Their parents didn't fully grasp that they were also repressing their voices, trapping thoughts and internal text bubbles that had no exit, because their parents didn't fully understand how to create and nurture dialogue that would fulfill the emotional needs of the child. They were learning as we all are. Due to the notorious and inhumane invention of slavery and racism by the **"US"** our elders and ancestors did many things from a space of fear and need to keep their children safe. Each generation has created survival mechanisms and behaviors in response to the environment and era, that eventually become unhealthy and unnecessary for the generations to follow.

This is our tipping point.

As energy goes it flows and if energy is not being released it becomes trapped. Hence the moment in the movie when the therapist says to Adelaide's (Lupita Nyong'o) parents, "She needs to sing, dance, write. Anything that can help her tell us her story." Adelaide overhears this conversation, and later in her teenage years becomes a great dancer. It's a moment of celebrated grace, glorified in the gift of expression. Amongst the shadow world, mirroring the seeming order is the underground world of tunnels that house our other selves.

How many of **"US"** have a shadow that is hungry for expression, struggling to organize the phonetics to pronounce a simple word? A side that many do not know exists. A part of glory that we let melt away over time. How many of **"US"** have shadows that don't get to say what they really want to say, because the fear of what people think about your authentic truth may be too much to handle? I know lawyers who stopped rapping, because the work of **"US"** has drowned the space and time for creativity to fully manifest through their beings. I know electricians who breakdance on the level of touring background dancers that the **"US"** pays to watch, but can no longer do it because the **"US"** has bills that need to be paid through collective debt.

"Recently through therapy I'm learning how to honor my inner child more and more each day. My inner child has a way of getting my attention." - @GregCorbinSpeaks

We all have an inner-child that is looking through our lens, scared of this big amazing world. As we grow older we are taught to believe our childhood doesn't matter, because acting like a child won't pay bills, help provide shelter, and other things. In reality our childhood experience inside the **"US"** shapes our adulthood and if there is a disconnect between the many personalities we have within it can grow fractured and unorganized. The **"US"** teaches us to leave behind, ignore and neglect the things that bring us joy. Recently through therapy, I'm learning how to honor my inner child more and more each day. My inner child has a way of getting my attention. Whether it's a cluttered desk, disorganized backseat, a chest filled with anxiety, foot tapping on the floor without my noticing; it knows what to do. It's teaching me lessons that my adult person has perspective and experience to absorb and learn. Through meditation I've been able to slow myself and my world down long enough to make internal connections and produce dialogue within that is bringing wisdom forth.

"We are not made of atoms. We are made of stories."

- Muriel Rukeyserk

The children are the warning. Their responses to the world we are building in the **"US"** serves as indicators of what's working and what's not working. The previous generations house much wisdom and knowledge that isn't being carried forth, because there aren't enough bridges being built between generations. It's one thing for a person to lose their voice, or never even have one. It's another for generations to collectively lose their voice, their story, because simply put as the great Muriel Rukeyserk once said, "We are not made of atoms. We are made of stories." 5 We are collectively losing our stories, our voice, our narrative while getting swallowed up by the mechanisms of the **"US."** The lack of humility and celebrated arrogance across the board is a key issue. None of us, no matter the age or background know it all. We all have something to offer. We need more spaces where dialogue and interface occurs. A place where voices are shared and celebrated, not submerged in the ego of the way the story should be or was. A cross referencing of possibility, so that innovative nuances can be honored and possibility can flourish through imagination. We have to create collective reflection points where we can see one another in one another. If we don't get **"US"**. The climate will get **"US"**. As above, so below.

This is our tipping point.

May we move forward in the name of humility, not insecure arrogance. May we create more intersections where the cross referencing of possibility and imagination flourish.

I do wonder what the movie settings would have looked like if it happened in a more urban environment. Imagine if the film was set in a city such as Chicago, Philadelphia, Houston, and even places that aren't in the **"US"** such as London, Tokyo, Lagos, and Rio De Janeiro. Imagine the scene of the shadow world with millions of people in a cone created area.

Unfortunately, this was best practice in some Black households, in which the residue formed racism and oppression.

Our inner children have interior decorators within them.

Children will always be the ones embodying prophecy with their responses to what we aim to teach, conditioned them into.

If we don't take care of **"US"** we will be devoured by **"US"**. What would happen if all our shadows came out all at once to play? The **"US"** has a collective shadow dwelling in inside the underbelly of an amplified scarcity consciousness

Of the Tethered (Shadow) people in the movie. Lupita's is the only one who can speak phonetically and produce words. The other tethereds aren't able to.

It is a tipping point that will involve self reflection and stillness. No matter how fast we have been trained to respond to our capitalistic conditions and transactional relationships, we must find time, create space to slow down and listen to our internal selves, our whole being. We all must step back from the noise, stretch to become more mindful, for the disorganization within will cause scattered outcomes and expressions. We all young and old, need to slow down, go inward, practice mindfulness and other stillness arts to become more aware of the roots underneath our behaviors.

The closer we get to the shadow the more we can shine our light.
As Above. So Below.
Inner **space**; Outer space.
Inner Climate; Outer Climate.
Light; **Dark.**

IMAGINATION IS YOUR SUPERPOWER. IT IS YOUR MAGIC.

@GregCorbinSpeaks

(BUY THE T-SHIRT)

Teaching

Ode to the Teachers

The way you move with flexibility,
nimble foot,
twisting like an intellectual gymnast for the future,
the future be the youth,
strategically implementing treasured lessons,
seeds of knowledge meant to shine in the chest of the mind,
utilizing different learning styles to invoke challenge towards
education,
you transform the auditory into the kinesthetic with movement
based activities,
supporting the adjustment of the tactile learner into the visual,
your **lessons are blessings** and each one residual,
exponentially growing in the future generations generations,
always on your toes ready to throw an audible in a field of dreams,
navigating classroom moods with a tone of tenacity and calm in
your tongue,
raising your voice at times because the **future is bright**,
and sometimes they need to be reminded,
that they are the sunshine the world will need in order to raise its
vibration,
so be the elevation, the climb,
thick oxygen taking up space while sharing the impact of
possibility,
grow those rooted seeds with branches of imagination,
 that the gardens did not even know they had,
be the constant reminder that purpose and empowerment take a
work ethic to accomplish, that nothing happens overnight,
show them the **power of delayed gratification and patience**,
and never be afraid to call the households that hold the future,
because we are waiting for them to answer the call,
in gratitude and grace,
thank you for your offering, it is **salvation**.

I've Been Both Of You

I recently witnessed a student and teacher have an eye-opening back and forth. Both of them were Black males. I just happened to be close enough to the conflict to intervene. I pulled the student to the side, spoke to him briefly and then accessed his emotional state. The student was not supposed to be in the class I found him in and was actually supposed to be in the classroom next door where we were holding our leadership development course. I noticed the teacher at *his* door, nonchalantly implying a surprising lack of care for the student's feelings/that I don't care how you feel. The student was ushered away to the dean of students. Towards the end of the class, he was permitted back inside the room. During a conversation about generational wealth he asked a surprising question, "Have you ever cursed at a teacher?" and I was in awe. Only minutes before that moment, he was threatening to bring his father up to the school. It made me think about where all this comes from and if this student is that aggressive when asking his father for advice, help with homework, or support on time management.

I answered his question with an honest answer. "Look, I've been both of you. I'm in both positions. I've been the teacher agitating the student, because I felt disrespected and embarrassed. And I've been the students cursing at the teacher in frustration that I was not getting my way. Maybe not as belligerent, but I've definitely mumbled at teachers and thrown insults. I've been both of you."

I realized that's why I was able to calmly intervene, because I had already experienced both positions. This allowed me to be empathetic for both involved. It's always about the backstory. It is a must that we move forward remembering that we are all carrying something. We all have baggage, some bags deeper working than others.

Later on I spoke with the teacher, and he shared that he had been going through a lot. It's not just the disrespect that is a catalyst for

90

response, but the type of energy we respond with. We have to make a significant choice as educating practitioners to understand the backstory of our students. The most important story is the backstory we carry everyday. That's right! We all have script and if we do not spend substantial time with self, then it's easy to lose ourselves in these emotionally charged moments.

It's sad to say when we make mistakes there will be some who do not care. Their willingness to practice emotional labor for others is unavailable, because they can barely carry the emotions they've created on their own. As working adults, politics and business dictate that people do what's in their best interest. Like I told the educator, be wary that you could be disposed of due to the capitalistic self preserving mentality and environment you work in. In other words, cover your ass and understand if a parent decides their child is in the right and causes enough havoc, you can easily be removed. We as human beings have to become more mindful of the many variables that write our internal script, which is archived in the subconscious mind.

Throwing Shade (Colorism)

ONE DAY while walking with some family members on Philadelphia's South St., I said, "I love those light skin girls with that long hair. They look beautiful."

It bounced off my 15-year-old tongue effortlessly, landing in the eardrums of my aunt.

She quickly responded, "Oh you like those light girls. You one of those House Niggas. That's what your name is. House Nigga."

My jaw dropped as I tried to win my Black Card back. "I didn't mean it like that!"

I was young and already walking the streets with a color complex constructing my attraction to girls based on the shade of their skin. My aunt called me "House Nigga" for the next 10 years, constantly helping me relive that moment. I was influenced by the images in my environment, mainly from television screens and magazines. I thought back to that moment on South Street last week while I was reading the Willie Lynch letter to a group of students in a classroom. The conversation was nothing short of intense.

"Have you all seen the stuff on social media where people are posting 'Team Dark Skin' and 'Team Light Skin?'

Nearly all of the students said yes.

"Ok. I got it," I said. "Y'all know about it. How do y'all feel about it?"

"I don't like being dark skin," one of them said. "I know I'm black. I just feel so heavy with blackness. I just don't like being black. In the summer it's the worst. I turn into the Grim Reaper."

His words turned the room into a quiet asylum. There was no

92

refuge from the words he had just shared. After years of teaching, I am sad to say his words did not shock me, but the boldness with which he spoke them did. With his face wrinkled in disgust he pointed to his skin, barely wanting to touch his arms while expressing his disdain for his tone. We watched him as his self-esteem was being placed in a coffin of hatred.

Another student said, "I don't like light skin people because they are stuck up and conceited. They think they better than us. When I was pregnant I said to my stomach don't let this baby come out light skin. Don't you know that baby came out light skin? I was mad!! Until the baby got a lil' chocolate a couple months later."

The students' laughter bellowed against the walls. I whispered a muted anger blended with frustration inside.

I then read actress Lupita Nyong'o's words: "I tried to negotiate with God. I told him I would stop stealing sugar cubes at night if he gave me what I wanted. I would listen to my mother's every word and never lose my school sweater again if he just made me a little lighter. But, I guess God was unimpressed with my bargaining chips, because I never woke up lighter."

The classroom fell silent once more, this time like an atomic bomb of reality had just mushroomed up, destroying all we knew. We sat staring at one another with a new beginning. All of us. It was an unexpected moment of silence. A moment where I could no longer hear the term, "House Nigga." Just the wheels of learning - turning at breakneck speeds.

We have to teach these young people how to love, how to dream, how to plan, and how to archive before it is all lost. We even have to teach them to love themselves.

The discreditation of blackness is deeply ingrained in these young people, and as we strive to hold on to the heritage, culture and self-love we have left, it's imperative we show our children that the value of their person should not be determined by the shade of their skin. That value comes when you discover your personal power and cherish every breath you have...

#BlackIsBeautiful #DarkSkinned
#LightSkinned #LearnedBias
#MicroAgression

Who Said It?

Writing Prompt: Write down the best and worst thing ever said to you.

Student's eyes begin to wander as their brains, their experiences make me smile, laugh, cry, cringe, practice spark a fire that spreads across the room. You can feel the heat from their minds as pens and pencils begin inscribing the imagery of their past. As they write I pace slowly around the room checking in with each student to make sure they know support is never far away. The flames they write are jumping off the pa silence, and ask questions.

"Times up. Finish that last line you are writing," I say gracefully as I pace around the room.

After taking a peek I instantly understand once again how any of these children can become an inferno searching for a cooling agent of peace.

Who would like to share first?

The flames sound like this:

"You ain't never going to be shit!"
Who said it?
"My teacher from 5th grade."

"You're having a little baby boy"
Who said it?
"The Doctor."

"You're a menace to society."
Who said it?
"The Judge."

"I love you so much. Please remember that always."
Who said it?
"My Mother."

"If I had a gun I would shoot you in the face."
Who said that?
"My Mother"

I hold my heart close simultaneously giving it to them. The gravity of each word settles in like a rock at the bottom of an ocean. An ocean of life experiences that offer themselves up in this very moment to solidify the power of words. It is a blessing that I've been chosen to create a brave and safe space for their minds that house a garden of secrets. Each thought helps us harvest from the soil of salvation.

On When To Hit Record

It's 11:35 a.m. The first lunch period is ending. The noise erupts from lava lit tongues spewing insults. Two fiery female students are gravitating closer to one another. The flames are spreading like wildfire as their peers feed off the energetic chaos. This promises not to end in peace. We are told as educators to never break up fights, because we could be hurt. That's also a way of protecting the educational system from lawsuits. The fire is spreading, though.

Today, I've decided to be water.

The fight didn't disturb me. It was the fact that students pulled out phones to record a moment of self-destruction and violence. If we didn't stop the fight, then the recordings would've landed on the internet in seconds, a celebration of fights and video and the hate that connects them.

Access to that type of power is a beast. It is a power driven by a culture that promotes attention-seeking behaviors by counting 'likes' and 'followers.'

There were at least 50 students entertaining the drama, because some people love conflict. Maybe it's all the guns, violence, blood and death that help layer the foundation of the country we live in.

There were no red lights to stop this traffic jam, just the flood of love and compassion overflowing from my heart. It's a heart that doesn't want to see anyone hurt—a heart that is an aquarium of hope that this would end peacefully.

While parting the crowd like an ocean, I noticed some students had phones out recording the conflict instead of being peacemakers. Fights and video go together now, creating a fire that laughed and antagonized the girls to clash. There was smoke, but thankfully, another student decided to be water too and assisted me in stopping the fire. The anger danced on their faces as they shouted obscenities.

Where does this fire come from? Where does the fire end?

97

When I was young we weren't the quickest to break up fights either, but we didn't have technology behind us, pushing a value system perpetuated by popularity that you can actually measure. It's hard to digest a world where people actually will record violence and death before they will go get help.

It wasn't always this way.

Eulogy For Brother Edgar

I didn't even know it was coming. I tried to do the dishes continuously washing the pain and sadness clean. It didn't work. Tear after tear draped down my face as I grew speechless. Choking on my words as I tried to process the message from Billy Joel which played on *Pandora* earlier today that "only the good die young." I cried for about 30 minutes after finding out Brother Edgar Mitchell passed away.

> "HE ALWAYS FOUND WAYS TO VALIDATE THE POSITIVE AND DISCOVER GOLD IN THE NEGATIVE." -
> @GREGCORBINSPEAKS

I received the word from my sis Zahrah Aya who i thank so much for calling and telling me over the phone so social media would not tell me first. My girlfriend with her healing soul comforted me and rubbed my back giving me a safe space to grieve and release.

His integrity, character and wisdom was unmatched. He was always there to talk with. I learned so much from watching him mentor, teach, and speak. He always found ways to validate the positive and discover gold in the negative.

His spirit was infinite with a calm demeanor that said "don't sweat that." He was a great father, husband, brother, teacher who did it all for the children.

For the students.
For the future.
For the universe.

His spirit was that of a healer. Each teardrop was a prayer sending his spirit peacefully home, forgiving this early departure for it is something that I anger over and choose to understand. That we will not be here forever, but while we are here we have a job to do. His spirit. His love. It was divine and it will be missed.

#RIP Edgar A Mitchell Jr

Emoting Lava

Unfortunately there are many young men and boys who are taught they shouldn't cry, as if vulnerability is a weakness. Yet, there are moments when emotional fences need to be up. Many from urban arenas where the concrete jungle is full of prey and predators learn there are times when the safest thing to do is to withhold emotions. Especially emotions that may expose a person's humanity. In an animalistic environment where the lack of resources creates desperation attached to scarcity and a frayed perspective of self worth, many are yearning for an outlet.

Some are speaking the language of their surroundings and not what's in their hearts. I find that many young people lack the ability to articulate their feelings, in fear that their emotional state will be neglected. It would be hard to survive and thrive in a world where people cry over everything, but when you no longer know how to emote and express your being, that is a problem. The heart becomes volcanic from the repression and suppression of one's feelings. This can become one of the worst forms of oppression a person can experience. This molten lava can become explosive, causing eruptions, spilling out onto other individuals. For some, that is all they have, fences. There is no bigger form of prison than the disconnection one may have with their emotions. We have to establish and develop more ways to show young men that emotions do not mean you're weak. It simply means you're human and more than your gender.

Emotions are simply energy in motion and it is imperative that we teach not just young boys and men, but all individuals the intelligence of their emotions, for knowledge and awareness is key. and unprivileged.

A Personal Space Odyssey

Driving around today was uncomfortable, humid, stuffy and oppressive as the Sun beacons its heat wavy intentions on the City Of Brotherly Love and myself. As I pulled up to park I noticed some of the young boys playing along with one young lady. One of the boys kept putting his hands in her face and swinging at her, as if he was play-fighting. I was instantly disturbed and unnerved.

The young lady spoke up, "leave me alone! I don't like you!!"

This seemingly frustrated the boy as he continued to swing ghost punches at the girl pushing to antagonize her even more. It was beyond the early stages of street harassment. It was the shadows of domestic violence that many young boys and girls learn at an early age. What is seen as fun and playing is becoming the norm. I even remember doing similar things when I was a child, but when I was told I was playing too much I stopped.

This young boy, who was only 9 years old did whatever it took to agitate the young lady even more. At one point he took both of his hands and grabbed her by the shoulders, as he tried to knee her. At this point I'm thinking of becoming the closest thing to a Father in the vicinity.

I don't know if he had a Father, but my Father and my Mother raised me to never put my hands on a female. Ever. I remember my Father saying, "You don't hit girls. Men that hit women are cowards."

She eventually opened her palm, extended her arm, placed it on his entire face and pushed forcefully to create space.

Space.

The importance of personal territory. Something that human beings need for comfort and more importantly, safety.

Eventually, the girl constantly asked him to leave her alone. She ran after, kicking him in the legs. The other boys kept on playing with smiles on their faces as if nothing was going on. As if nothing was wrong. But with all the media they are exposed to that degrades and objectifies women, would you find anything wrong with it either? Maybe not.

Not to mention they may have seen this on the street or in their households. As the young girl ran it reminded me of anything but child's play. Her face, frustrated and flustered with each expression screaming, "I didn't ask for this." His face bent in aggression, persistence and vengeance, as if he didn't initiate the series of events.

At this moment, I was getting out of the car. I overheard the conversation as other boys called another young girl d***head, d***eater and other explicit names that do not reflect the highest good of female energy in our universe.

Internally, I was thinking these three things:
"Where did they learn this?"
"Who taught them this?"
"How would they feel if this were their sister or even their mother?"

I instantly called the young boy over and the convo flowed like this:

"Hey youngan! Come here." My face stern and stable with focus. "What's your name?"

He said, "Jamir."

How old are you?

"I'm 10."

"Why are you putting your hands on that young lady like that?"

"Because she hit me!"

"Are you sure, because that's not what I witnessed. You were swinging at her and trying to kick her. What was that about?

Jamir sucks his teeth

And I say, "Jamir. I'm not mad at you. You can look at me.

His head still staring at the ground as if this was the only way he knew how to deal with disappointment.

I continue, "I'm not perfect and I did similar things when I was your age, and it is not right. You hear me?"

"Yes. *His head still aimed at the ground. Jamir still struggled to look me in my face the entire time.*

"How would you feel if someone did that to your sister?"

"I don't have a sister."

"Well, what if you had a sister or what if someone did that to your Mother? How would you feel?

"I would be mad"

"Well, think about that the next time you think it's ok to put your hands on girls. That's not ok. It looked unsafe. Imagine how she felt. She looked scared and uncomfortable. How would you like it if some did that to you?"

"I wouldn't."

"Man listen. I'm not mad at you in any way. But I want you to be the best person you can be. Please do better not just for yourself but everyone in your community. There is too much violence."

"I understand." Jamir's head shook in a gentle understanding and he walked off.

Friends asked him who I was.

At that moment I decided to be someone who cared. I wasn't interested in comfort zones and rejection. I had to speak up, because my mature adult mind saw the repercussions of the moment. Domestic violence starts very early and we have to do better about curbing these behaviors with preventative measures. Our youth are the sum measures of everything the world gives them and we have to take hold of what's poured into them. It takes a village. In that village model we have to become interveners and disruptors of what we do not want to see in the world. This is the work. It is not always fun games and glory. It is challenging and uncomfortable. Yes, driving around today was uncomfortable, but not as uncomfortable as witnessing or being the young lady who was being tormented by misguided behavior and bad habits.

It's hard to digest a world where people actually will record violence and death before they will go get help.

ASK THE QUESTION YOU ARE AFRAID TO ASK.

@GregCorbinSpeaks

(BUY THE T-SHIRT)

Father

Wind Chimes For My Father

There's immense pressure in being a father figure for our youth.
I am moved to do this work, feeling as if it may be my duty.
A root of purpose meant to sprout into impact.

"It takes a village to raise a child, and to raise a family." - @GregCorbinSpeaks

There were many times my father took my childhood friends to the movies or basketball courts with us. Those memories sing like wind chimes on a back step while bird watching for an ancestor. Those experiences sneak in from time to time, reminding me it takes a village to raise a child, and to raise a family. When my father passed away from lung cancer, a close friend, a brother of mine wrote a letter thanking my father for his ability to be a father figure. His words resonated throughout the entire space, and broke me into tears.

Youth who are seeking hope and possibility in you.

It's difficult to fill their gaping wounds.
It's difficult to fill their gaping wounds.

Wounds that can be gently soothed but not healed, healed by a surrogate father until they are mature enough to understand the circumstances that might have made their father who they are and who they will become.

And even after understanding this,
it's still challenging to relinquish the hurt and harm caused by a fathers absence.

It's difficult to fill their gaping wounds.

It's difficult to fill their gaping wounds.

I will never forget what someone said to me during my father's transition. It was a grey haired elder and his nephew. The nephew said, "Here's my father. And no he isn't my biological father, but he is my father. I feel your pain. At least you had a father, because some don't." This conversation intertwined with the experiences of my father are the wind chimes on the back step. Thank you Dad.

"At least you had a father, because some don't."

Hands

My father was great with his hands,
an uncanny ability to fix anything a house could hold.
If the front wall was falling apart
he would grab bricks,
and stir cement with water hose water.

I love those water hose moments.

My father was a stern man, intelligent, constantly learning,
teaching himself
how to fix anything
his hands were willing too.

My father was a trilateral commission,
street smart
philosopher.

A Carpenter's Hands

When you lose an engaged parent it becomes the catalytic experience for recognition of impact. It becomes an instant source for reflection. The grieving process is an opportunity to identify what parts of you will live on through your example of living. In January, my father's birthday passed. He transitioned almost 17 years ago.

Lately I've been dwelling on the departure of a man that taught me many things. He was the king of self reliance, willing to teach himself anything needed to keep the house together. As a child I remember my parents keeping books in the weirdest locations. There was even a set of books in the hallway lined up against a bannister.

One of the books was a 3 inch thick, grey and red auto mechanic guidebook. It could teach someone interested anything they wanted to know about a car. My father loved cars. Cadillacs and Oldsmobiles were his main choices. We had a grey Oldsmobile '98, originally made in '83. And boy would that car have some challenges. My ever so frugal father would read through that auto mechanics guidebook to learn how to fix the brakes, the carburetor, the radiator, the catalytic converter, the hinges on the door, and pretty much anything that needed fixing. This was my father's way of being in control.

Early on in my life he said, "don't pay someone something to do something you can do for yourself". That is to say he wasn't the delegating type (which I've definitely absorbed in some productive and non productive ways).

And it wasn't just the car. He could repair anything in the house, from the front wall holding back the soil in the garden (really grass and a miniature evergreen tree) to the porch railings and the roof. See, my father was built by a generation that wasn't given grace. A generation that watched its martyrs become martyred and saw an unsettling drug addiction find alcohol and other hard drugs. A generation that saw domestic abuse outsourced by plantation pain, the ravage of racism and wars that pimped the patriarch into drafts that needed to be dodged.

Yes, the years that helped construct my father's identity were layered with the threat of local gang violence, dealing with an abusive father and a city with a racist mayor, perpetuating a cycle of abuse.

Transparency

For Parents and Children

I recall being punched in the face by a childhood friend over a football. After it happened, I ran in the house crying to my parents:

My Father asked "what are you crying for?!"

I shared with my parents what just happened in the streets. ███████ just punched me."

My Father stated, " Go hit him back!"

I wanted no smoke! I was crying hysterically. My Father tried to push me back out there. It didn't work. The panic and terror from the possible conflict amplified my crying.

My Mother jumped in, "Why are you doing that to that boy?"

I felt scared, nervous, anxious and disappointed in that moment. Years later, I would experience conflict and bullying, but would be afraid to share the insights with my Father.

That one moment and choice of his parenting, which he learned from somewhere else created a dynamic in our relationship that would craft many conversations that never happened. I would get bullied and be afraid to tell my Father what was happening, because I didn't want to be a disappointing son.

Later, my parents would enroll me in martial arts, but it didn't last long. I was still walking in fear in school environments. I haven't really been able to see how much this has impacted me until I seriously committed to THERAPY.

My Father missed some great opportunities to nurture me through experiences, because he lacked the ability and tools to navigate certain experiences. Unfortunately, my silence didn't allow some of those conversations to manifest. The little 7 year old inside is still angry with his Father. He loves him so much, but it's complex.

Later in life I would replicate similar behaviors in the classroom, with my foster son, and nephews. I've learned to forgive myself, while pushing myself to understand the damage it can cause. The sins of generations can easily be replicated in oppressive manners.

As a full adult, I truly understand why my Father would encourage me to defend myself. We lived in a drug ridden neighborhood built by the crack epidemic, which spiked crime, family breakdown, police brutality and violence of all sorts. My Father, a survivor of gang war, poverty, gunshot wounds and more carried his own trauma. When he was encouraging me to fight back it was about survivability in a neighborhood that was strategically disposed and designed to become the source of economic stimulus and job creation for others across the system.

The building of prison, justification of social systems, and more was at stake. I still recall witnessing Mothers and Fathers become drug users, prostitutes, hustlers and more. I'm not defending my Father's choice at that moment, but I do see the reality that he would not always be around to save or protect me from what the streets and schools and the world would offer, and boy did they provide some experiences. My Father was a product of his era and his generations challenges, successes, trauma, healings and more.

I forgive you Dad, and forgive the generations before you that did not know any better. You still were awesome. Love you Dad.

I forgive myself for beating up on myself for feeling powerless, hopeless and incompetent. I forgive myself for my own shortcomings. Love you Lil Greg and Big Lil Greg (as my Uncles would say .

I'm a better human being today than I was yesterday because I'm sitting still with myself more. Studying myself more. Therefore, I've been dedicating time to strengthening my conflict resolution skills, restorative justice practices and wisdom, and increasing my knowledge on emotional intelligence to cut down impulsive behaviors that lead to violence.

So far the workshops I've been teaching nationally on Hip Hop, Wellness, Healing Justice and Restorative Practices have provided a space for authenticity as an educator and practitioner. I am walking deeper into my path of what I always knew. I'm a Healer, a Griot and Teacher of many practices.

Father's Day

I miss asking my father for advice.
I miss exchanging the wisdom from books we both read.
I miss the sound of his voice.
I miss the stink smell of his magic shaving cream.
I miss the smiles we shared.
I miss those semi-corny semi funny jokes.
I miss the pranks and laughter.
I miss the character building sessions called
fatherhood.

I miss saying happy Father's Day and you saying thank you, I love you.
                          I miss you.

I love you dad and thank you
for everything you have taught me,
for everything you have given me and
for everything you have shown me.

I was riding with my father around our neighborhood. It was somewhere close to the Broad and Olney transportation depot for SEPTA. We were riding down Olney Ave when we saw two guys trying to rob this college student from Lasalle University. My father pulled the car over and with no hesitation jumped out the car and ran over to the scene of the crime. The would-be thieves ran off angry, disgusted that they couldn't get anything off the student before my father came.

They threatened him, "We gon see you again ole head. I should shoot you." *As one of them postured and acted as if he was grabbing a gun"*

I remember seeing the guy grab for a gun. The fear shock-waved through my whole being.

For a split second I was scared I was going to lose my father.

My father responded, "You ain't gonna do nothing."

I was right behind my father at the age of 16, trying to back him up and hold it down for him. He said, **"What are you doing, get back in the car."** And I don't know what made me get out of the car more. Was it loyalty or the fear of something terrible happening to my father? We live in times where people witness crime and never speak up, hear a young woman being abducted while screaming for help and no one responds, or the daily recording of school fights as self destruction becomes the norm of entertainment.

Yes, times are different and what my father did that day was risky, selfless, thoughtful, brave, and impactful. But if we don't start being more focused on unity and seeing ourselves in others, then we will continue to ride this track. Watching him then instilled certain values in me that I can never relinquish. Especially not after what I saw growing up. I'm blessed to have the parents and the examples they have instilled in me. Their investment was not just for their own profit, but a wider community of people. Make sure people know what they mean and can do so much more for their communities. For my father, my hero, my example of selfless communal activism. His intentions were always pure, loving and thoughtful. When you see me, you see him. That simple! He wasn't just a positive Black Man. He was a positive human being.

Love you POPS!

I'm Building A Loveletter For My Son
From Greg Sr.

In 2001 it became apparent that I was taking spoken word poetry seriously. I was part of a poetry collective called **"The Ghettohero Supaman Savapoets"**, with my friends Jonifin Marvin *(Inglish aka The Getaway Driver)* and DonCarlos *(DutchMasta aka Suga Tongue Slim)*. It was a great name. In all honesty we were trying to be creative and different. We knew that the right kind of "different" combined with talent would make us memorable.

Together we created an event called "Kryptonite" which we promoted on neon green flyers during the sizzling summer of 2001, leaving them on car windows and in storefronts. Ironically the location, Pearl of Africa located on the 600 block of South Street had no stage. We agreed to ask my father to build a stage for our open mic arts event "Kryptonite" in which he said "yes." During a four hour stretch on a 97 degree day, a stage was built.

While my Father sawed wood and hammered nails, I didn't know that he was battling stage four lung cancer. After his transition in July 2002, it would become clear that the stage wasn't just a message about building a foundation for your children. It was also a love letter.

A love letter for his son.
Greg Jr.
aka Just Greg

I'm Building A Loveletter For My Son

For my son Noble

I am building a love letter
a carefully constructed prayer of gratitude
a timeless whisper leaning in the shadows of eternity
a passionate statement of legacy
it will be an unforgettable replica of purpose robed in dignity
hammered into the platform of potential

I am building a love letter
it will be a dedication
a prominent prototype
written in the script of life
written in blood, sweat, tears and a main ingredient, love
each precipitating drop of soul that drowns itself into the wood
will be a conversation built with the body language of best wishes
vital support   a striving perseverance   unbroken
promises
this love letter will pay homage to every breath breathing in the
future
it will have roots that run deep into the course of family trees
birthrights branching out to touch the entire globe
generation by generation
leaving an impact that the world will feel endlessly
reading the love letters of our family lineage
Son, this stage is for you and I look forward to the love letters you
will build.

Confessions Of A Poet

My First Poem

I've seen people primarily get involved with poetry in three ways. They have a crush on someone, they want money or they simply just love writing. Now of course there is more. When I first arrived on the spoken word poetry scene, it was about expression, meeting new people, and compensating for the challenges I had with writing rhymes. I fell in love with it fast, entrenched with communicating thoughts and ideas. My first poem was about my anger for racism and how I was often mistreated at the predominantly white college I attended on the main line outside of Philadelphia. I was nervous as I stood in front of strangers in a nightclub on a Sunday afternoon, with a cut off basketball league shirt on. I believe it was from the "Untouchables League," located at 29th and Clearfield. I had my cargo pants on. Oh, how I love cargo pants. I worked my way through the poem, stumbling on each word, reading from a book as my hands trembled, channeling nervous energy into a cacophony of expression.

Emotionally invested in justifiable anger, I found an audience of fifty plus people, who unselfishly transformed their eardrums into empathy and compassion. I was somewhat desensitized from the pain of events until I read the poem, in which the trapped energy (emotion) was unlocked. As a 21 year old young man and burgeoning poet, I lacked the emotional intelligence and self awareness to sit with my thoughts mindfully in meditation. It was easier for me to focus on the anger, rage, hurt, suffering and pain. Through expression of spoken word, I learned quickly that the right formula of political consciousness, truth telling, humor and wit could win you an applause or ovation, which in a capitalistic society means approval. Approval transforms into influence and influence potentially becomes groupthink. I found myself getting lost in the game of people pleasing behaviors that are often placed on the shoulders of artists.

Trauma informed was not the identity of my generation. Our identity was more along the lines of resilient workaholics who believed with a college degree you could win. For the most part my peers were trauma ignorant. We only heard the word trauma when we watched television shows about hospitals. Other than that, the word trauma was not in the vocabulary of myself or my peers. The concept had yet to drip into the mainstream and as a result, trigger warnings (and other consideration skills) were not in practice. Through deep meditation and amplified awareness activities I've been able to recall the previous life and experiences I had in the poetry community.

"Each time I speak I am healing that little child in the back of the classroom. I am teaching him to value his thoughts, his voice and himself. Each time I perform I am teaching him how to love his voice again and again and again."

- @GregCorbinSpeaks

There are moments when I didn't even notice I was acting out, performing life through my trauma. I had no clue of this until recent times. The applause and approval worked perfectly for that inner child still seeking to prove himself to the cool kids. The stage was a perfect place for the child trapped in the silence of his own insecurity, sitting terrified in the back of class, afraid the bullies would threaten him with shame. Each time I speak I am healing that little child in the back of the classroom. I am teaching him how to value his thoughts, his voice and himself. Each time I perform I am teaching him how to love his voice again and again and again.

124

All Eyes On Me

The attention economy of the poetry scene is no different than any other art form where eyes are locked in on you. I remember writing poems that didn't receive the applause that was matched by the previous poem's applause and scratching the poem to the realm of non-existence, because my approval ratings dropped. I didn't think about variables, or the mere fact that when people like your verbal artistic expressions, it's more about them, than it is about you. It's validating their perspective and personal experiences. Truthfully, I thought about being accepted, so if my poem didn't receive the applause, I felt rejected at my core. I would go home sad, motivated to write the piece that was going to topple the system, but in reality I was motivated to write the poem that was going to fill the addiction.

> "YES IT WAS PROFITABLE, BUT IT WAS A TRAP. THE PERFECT TRAP FOR SOMEONE LIKE ME. THE PERFECT STAGE BECAME A CAGE..." - @GREGCORBINSPEAKS

I was looking for a hit. I was becoming a narcissist, quickly learning to work rooms in the form of manipulation. I was losing myself in the motives of popularity and trauma under the disguise of people pleasing behaviors, aware that the increase in popularity leads to more demand for the supply. The supply was laced with an exposed pain body that enhanced trauma bonds with listeners, who proceeded to purchase my products. Listeners would approach me saying, "thank you for your courage, bravery, vulnerability." Yes it was profitable, but it was a trap. The perfect trap for someone like me.

The perfect stage became a cage in which the little chubby guy inside was locked in what seemed to be an eternal battle with self acceptance and image conscious behaviors.

"IT WAS ALL A PERFORMANCE. ONE THAT SWALLOWED MY JOY AND DISTURBED MY AUTHENTICITY AT TIMES." - @GregCorbinSpeaks

It was all a performance. One that swallowed my joy and disturbed my authenticity at times. I receive that I was never really sure of who I was, needed to be. Sometimes you have to get lost in something to find yourself. And maybe that is the best poem a person can perform.

Poetry Scene

The ground is shifting.
The weather cycle within
is swirling with transformation on its mind.
It's thinking about cleaning you out.

You're afraid of the storm.
It's an internal flood that is sweeping your soul clean,
purifying it from top to bottom.

It feels like you're drowning,
but you're really being notified of what the problem is,
so you can become
the solution.

Thank you Sis Ursula Rucker for teaching me how to write about the storm, while being the light. Track 19 on Illadelph Halflife pushed my mind and my pen. I appreciate you.

Hip-Hop

Hip-Hop: A Fine Art

Hip hop is a fine art that has surpassed the economic infrastructure of previous art forms, because it was born from a space of liberation birthed out of desperation. Its origin story, linked directly to oppressive experiences, is related to blues, jazz, bluegrass, rock and gospel.

There is an audience that overlooks the substantial impact of hip hop in how it invites everyone to the table. At times this invitation is a reluctant one, because people of color have struggled to own the right to their creative license.

Who owns the publishing rights to hip hop? Who owns the house rights to say they created it? Who owns the bragging rights?

When the Broadway phenomenon *Hamilton* debuted, the entire country, and eventual globe took notice. This wasn't just because it was celebrating the life of Alexander Hamilton, but because it was yet another way to carry the legacy of a historical figure that clouds the collective consciousness of American History. Rightfully so, no matter how you feel about the well woven racism in this society's foundation, Hamilton was indeed a brilliant man. And hip-hop was a brilliant vessel to carry his legacy.

It's More Than Hip-Hop

Hip Hop is a biochemical language that is expressed from a generated portal that transforms energy via emotion into word. The human anatomy works in tandem with energy absorbed from personal or empathic experiences in order to transmute it into a concrete form of sound and vibration. The sound and vibration in turn causes a chemical reaction rooted in the intention of the expresser. Therefore, sound healing or damage can occur based upon how we use this tool of verbal expression whether it be by song, poetry, dance and other forms of art. Each experience leaves an impression in which some are good and some are not so good. This is based upon the perception of the experiencer. In this way, HH powerfully possesses an ability to change an attitude, idea, thought pattern, or belief system while connecting to a source of healing or damage.

What would happen if language was weaponized to trigger a populace into verbal sensitivity movements, in which people couldn't say certain words because the catalytic response could cause such discomfort, an individual had to leave a certain space?

Yes, we should be more intentional with our language, but we must question what and who is deciding what is appropriate and what is not?

In recent times we have seen an uptick in *semantic warfare*. This has caused people to police others at a higher rate. When people are at odds, they become more focused on what they don't have in common, causing an environment where there is more division than unity. **It's more than hip hop.** Hip hop at its core is grassroots organizing, conflict resolution, and a peace building mechanism that can change environments one individual at a time.

Hip hop is energy work. It is the shift.

Blues Muse

Chicago "Drill Music" is blues. Just as blues as Muddy Waters.

Just as blue as cotton plantation lullabies.

Blues.

Hip-Hop 401: RIP _____

Still wrapping my head around how artists produce music and create capital off of societal ills and broken community issues that the listener finds a way to discover joy in - be it escape and/or cathartisism. .

Yesterday, a rapper by the name of _____who repped _____ squad was shot 15 times to death. _____ also had a mixtape entitled *Get Your Casket On* and *Hurry Up and Die*. In today's society, we forget that words are powerful and manifest some of the most beautiful and dangerous outcomes. Each word is derived from the breath of life and has the ability to transform into a divine or destructive experience. We have to watch what we say and say what we really mean. We can't continue to make songs about the behavior and not the root foundation of the problem and expect progress. Artists who come from impoverished neighborhoods have always created content that have either addressed the issues, brought awareness to the problems at hand, or created artists who instead of outgrowing their environment, chose to become consistent purveyors of communal behaviors.

It's difficult to find solutions in today's mainstream rap because complaining about the problem has a higher reward. Also, failing school systems aren't providing critical thought that may help young people discover productive solutions. It's a dumbed down curriculum, where creativity is being slaughtered, and hopelessness is birthed from a lack of innovation and boredom.

Therefore, we adapt. We become conditioned to the new norms of reactionary thought and behavior almost like flesh filled cyborgs living in a trance where we believe choice is available.

But it may not be?

The entertainment industry has been shifted to glorify violence of all kinds while listeners dance to it. That's like dancing to death especially when the words speak so much of it. Listen, I love *Mobb Deep*, *Biggie*, *2Pac*, *NWA*, because that's what was given to me by my environment. Yes, it was hyper violent, uber-masculine and super misogynist. That hasn't really changed much at all. But I also had intelligent parents and other supporters that helped me listen with a critical ear as they explained what the lyrics derived from and really meant.

I watched artists pour out their hearts in May (insert year) for _____. Some in anger speaking of how much he didn't deserve it. But it all stems to a systemic problem where genocide and the death of Black Men are a constant norm, in which someone is always making a profit as if each breath is tied to a past auction block. Prisons are feeding off this mentality of brokenness that many are conditioned to view as normal. We must shift that! A gunshot victim may generate up to two million dollars for the system. That's one person creating jobs and capital because of their life either being threatened or taken away. We must shift that. This is why we must reinvest, transform thinking, create spaces of transparency that celebrate healing and authenticity. Our value systems of what we reward are extremely off kilter and manipulated by record sales and other reward systems in the media industry.

Are we really dancing to a slow death? Is this really life? Some of the artists sharing condolences make similar music that _____ created as a conduit/vessel for his life experiences. He rapped about what he experienced, lived or watched others live through. As a (insert age) year old man he made some decisions in songs that didn't promote the best energy, but I truly understand where it came from and how it was created. Like many, _____ leaves behind loved ones that will cope in many different ways trying to seek an answer that only God/Allah could provide. Why do we go through these things? The lessons? The pain? It's so much.

It's sad how rappers rap about drugs/guns/violence and then fall victim to the same content they rap about. The tongue is powerful.

Hip Hop 501: RIP Stuart Scott

Dear Stuart Scott:

You were the cultural colloquialism dropped in the mainstream, leveraging your connection with hip hop. A revolutionary burst of innovation, stretching the imagination, leaving minds like land mines. **BOOYAH!!!!** In the context of broadcasting, you were the spell using spells to intel with innovative intelligence never seen on the scene. We could see the melanin magic sparkle on a lexicon drenched in your personal choice of words, choosing to be the chosen one in ways only hip hop could manifest. The only media persona utilizing catch phrases from a world many did not know existe. And if they did, they probably did not want it to, unless it benefited them. You made me dream of one day being a sportscaster. I mean, you even quoted Biggie, Jay, and Pac. **BOOYAH!!!!** You had this paradigm shifting cool. As you would state, *"as cool as the other side of the pillow."*

"As cool as the other side of the pillow."
- Stuart Scott [6]

You were one of my favorite poets with a quick wit for creative conjunctions, linking similes between culture and sports events. As a child, I taped Sportscenter not just for the highlights, but also because of the way you played with language. Your flow was battle rap worthy, as you showcased to so many Black youth that it was totally ok to be yourself. More than a diversity, equity and inclusion quota, you represented in ways only the spirit of hip hop rebellion could. **BOOYAH!!!!** And even when you battled cancer you had this profound courage to never know what stage you were in, as you picked up mixed martial arts to amplify your fight against a disease that has claimed too many. You were a light beam, beamed from satellite to satellite. Duplicating the impact and imprint of style, flavor and flare appearing on television screens everywhere and you will always be as cool as the other side of the pillow. **BOOYAH!!!!**

Affirmations 1

It's ok to "Slow Down."

Breathe.

Create space

       for you to process

       your thoughts

              and emotions.

"YOU ARE SOMEONE'S PROMISE AND YOU WERE NOT PUT HERE TO BE BROKEN."

@GregCorbinSpeaks

(BUY THE T-SHIRT)

Poems And Prose Interlude 1

Tears

Tears are liquid inner mountains
melting from the deepest abyss of the soul
ridge lined eyes turning maroon
a physical extraction
placid lake heartbeats leave an imprint
sound tracking a trail of humility
have you ever cried from your diaphragm
a release so buried it feels like an exorcism
spilling over from the power of being present
alive inside
the last time I cried
there was an ammunition I did not see coming
there is some(body) home
bloodshot eyes is evidence that there is residence
inside my rib cage.

inside my rib cage
bloodshot eyes is evidence that there is residence
there is some(body) home
there was an ammunition I did not see coming
the last time I cried
alive inside
spilling over from the power of being present
a release so buried it feels like an exorcism
have you ever cried from your diaphragm
placid lake heartbeats leave an imprint
sound tracking a trail of humility
a release so buried it feels like an exorcism
a physical extraction
ridge lined eyes turning maroon
melting from the deepest abyss of the soul
Tears are liquid inner mountains

Marriage

When you marry someone, you are making a divine contract with
your souls.
When you marry someone, you marry their relationship with
themselves,
their relationship with their trauma and their family dynamics.
You are marrying their good, their bad and their ugly.
And when you're doing marriage correctly
you realize there is nowhere to hide, or run,
because you realize your relationship
with yourself
is most
important.

Snapshots

Life is a collection of vibrant snapshots.
Each frame is a fitting voice in the song of a one heart continuum.
We all have been gifted with our own set of eyes,

cameras that have an astounding ability to zoom in and zoom out.
There will be moments when we must zoom out
and see the world of snapshots for what it is.

Frame by frame
we gather these photos
with hopes of being able to share our beautiful photography
in authentic ways.

There will be moments where we photobomb,
because at times we aren't sure we belong in the frames that life is
presenting us.
There will be moments we *don't* belong in and moments we *do*
belong in.

Fire

A conditioned and seasoned firefighter
I ran to put out the flames of others,
exhausting the fire that God granted me.

I've learned to pace myself,
to keep better boundaries
while shamelessly exercising them
without the haunting people-pleasing mentality.

We are awakening from the spells of the past.
Moving light years into the future with hearts full of light.

As we unearth shadows of our darkness.
We choose to let go and grow past our past, because it no longer
defines us.
We are the affirmation of humanity,
the ancestors promise to shed the dead and shine our melanin.

Life's A Stage And You Must Act

Life is a stage full of institutions containing race, religion, gender, sexual orientation, sex, class and more. Each one has different job descriptions inside of different job descriptions, roles that shape expectations that inform our character on this stage called life. ***They are descriptions; de "script"-ions.*** Each script full of directives, underlying objectives that internalized behaviors dictate. People learn these scripts as young people, the moment they are born through a process called socialization. Each institution comes with learned behaviors that are influenced by our everyday surroundings, filled with their own umbrellas in which behavior is at times homogenized and normalized. Key word here is "performance." If you go off script too far, you may lose people because it's outside of the box of expectations. If people get too uncomfortable, humans may face shame from other humans. This might happen at times when their subconscious minds are programmed to see institutional behavior in certain "scripted" ways, because people want what's comforting to them. So yes, the stage is set, the script is written and you must act.

YOU'RE ONLY TIRED BECAUSE YOU ARE CHASING THE THING THAT IS NOT MEANT FOR YOU.

@GregCorbinSpeaks

(BUY THE T-SHIRT)

Systems

The System

Humans are ripping each other apart at the seams. They are barreling for positions, yearning to be close to power and self preservation, dominating daily movements with attitude. Justifiably, there is a disgruntled angst boiling underneath our society. We need something to restore our humanity, before the art forms and necessary energies of compassion, grace, redemption and forgiveness dissolve more than they already have. All acts of love are breaths of the freshest air. But often we forget that oxygen is both a gift and a privilege. People are afraid. They are dwelling in depression. And this is a spiritual depression with *the Nothing* (apathy) arriving as scavengers are exploiting the pain of the suffering for cash. This is what the system teaches us all directly and indirectly. So we have to be the ones to create an ecosystem of love as solution centered beings who move in graceful peace and strength.

"Healing threatens capitalism."

- @GregCorbinSpeaks

We've mastered the art of dragging, but we must master the art of **picking others up**. We've mastered destruction, but we will master **construction**. We've mastered ripping things apart but we will master putting them back **together.** Fear has us obsessed with ourselves more than ever. When we realize this, then we can make strides. It's easy to let evil win. We must create and generate love from within and spread it.

Some people build their businesses around their anger, trauma and suffering. The mere thought and act of healing may threaten their ability to gain social capital, because it's attached to a brand that makes them money, but there is a cost. Sometimes miserable people pay for misery.

Healing threatens capitalism. There are profit margins attached to every wound. Business models making sure the corporation that is this country is working in the favor of chaos. Cities designed to engineer conflict, trapping trauma in pockets of people. As James Baldwin stated, "History is trapped in the people and the people are trapped in history." We choose to repeat it like a broken record of brokenness. Who will heal us if our healing may make us bankrupt? If the financial system breaks, it means there is still a soul to save.

"Dear America,

where is your soul?"

- @GregCorbinSpeaks

The Value System: This Time

For My Family

Truth is, the system is called capitalism for many reasons. One of them is to teach people a value system that is so drenched in materialism that it treats people as transactional objects rather than human beings. Many adopted that belief and manifested behaviors that were attached to provision. On one hand if someone isn't bringing home (enough) income the lights could go off, the roof may leak, the fridge may end up empty, and eventually homelessness could result. Time is what's needed most to cultivate a healthy and impactful family. Do we have enough time? Is there enough opportunity to be fully present with family?

The new (2019) economy doesn't care for that at all. In a society where speed is currency, things like patience and stillness become less valuable in places of employment. Certain environments, especially over populated cities where scarcity consciousness creates desperation and anxiety. The anxiety and stress shows up via overworked individuals who work tirelessly to fulfill the needs of the family. Hence, the next recession will put a strain on many family dynamics, because the need to work extra and save more may be vital for some to survive rather than thrive. Yes, those who create the value system dictate the ideas of success. And since materialism is a tool for compensating for the "idea of lack," we have to reconfigure a more productive value system. There are many layers.

"Are we chasing our past and calling it the future?" - @GregCorbinSpeaks

Growing up in an under resourced environment taught me how to be resourceful, resilient and innovative. It is because of my experience with poverty that I learned to utilize my imagination and

149

expand what was possible in my mind. As I evolve I have massive gratitude for what my upbringing taught me, while on the other hand I am shifting my relationship with time and money. I am detoxing the poverty mindset that thrives on "not enoughness and lack". It can block blessings, because the conditioning that green paper or any paper dictates your worth is such a limiting existence. If I continue to have an attitude of lack it triggers me to behave from the mindset of the past. Many of us do this. Are we chasing our past and calling it the future?

Time is the biggest asset a person can have. Time allows me to make eye contact with my wife, hold conversations in a productive manner during a moment of conflict, and while bouncing our son on my lap, because patience to listen is one of the most valuable assets you can have. And that comes with time.

The System: Drawing Lines

We live in a very charged and sensitive time, where gaslighting is used to provoke and evoke conflicting reactions. It's a moment in history where language is being used by groups and individuals to propagandize agendas. A moment where semantics can be altered, because each person is individually living in their own reality.

For example, you can be standing in a room of 20 people with different perceptions. Those 20 perceptions can simultaneously be 20 different realities. **That is 20 different "keeping it reals" or reels of a worldview that is influenced by experience, family dynamics, upbringing and traumatic events.**

The more information that is uncovered and unveiled, the more complex our everyday reality becomes. It's very easy for people to be divided these days. Our personal interests and conditioning for self preservation could lead us down a road of collective self destruction if we do not find a shared mission to coexist around. The moment someone doesn't agree they are being attacked verbally, on and off-line.

Lines in the sand are being drawn, mentally and geographically.

The culture of conflict is spilling over where the question, "can't we all just get along?," comes up consistently. And their answer is, "not like this". Not in a world where information is being used to build and destroy.

There is a purge happening.

Get your spirits right.
Get your hearts right.
- @GregCorbinSpeaks

We have inherited this world from those who came before us. This is about who controls the thinking of the populous, the flow of information, and the tools to manipulate minds towards division.

Building the house of freedoms with master's tools can never work, because it plays on the hurt. It feeds on ego and vulnerability, intermingling with the worst parts of humanity.

"Choose your leaders with wisdom and forethought.
To be led by a coward is to be controlled by all that the coward fears.
To be led by a fool is to be led by the opportunists who control the fool.
To be led by a thief is to offer up your most precious treasures to be stolen.
To be led by a liar is to ask to be told lies. 7
To be led by a tyrant is to sell yourself and those you love into slavery."
-Octavia Butler

The (School) System

I was fueled by my self righteous anger, frustration and in some ways, hatred for white people. I was raised through a public school system that did not deeply explore institutional racism and systemic oppression. It was designed to make sure I didn't. My first year in college was at a Predominantly White Institution (PWI) on the main line of Philadelphia. There were many moments where I experienced racism. A moment I will never forget was the day I was accused of cheating on a music test.

I arrive at the test site and make my way to the seat. Before today I was passing every test with anywhere from 90 to 100 points. I recall my intro to music class that lingered for weeks on Mozart, Beethoven, and other white people. The only section discussing the impact of black people in music is a section focusing on jazz and the blues. It lacks any mention of hip-hop, spoken word, or the heavy black influence on rock and roll. Whenever I raise a question about it in class I receive no answers. When I sit down at my desk I start pulling out my books and my pencil.

The teacher in the front of the class snaps at me and asks, "What are you doing? You can't do that. You can't have your stuff out. What are you doing?" I respond with a look of shock on my face, hold up my pencil and say, "I was looking for something to write with."

"Well, you can't have your notes out with your book out." I say, "I know I'm looking for something to write with."

I calmly put my books away waiting for the test to be passed around. I glance around and see nothing but a sea of white students with both their books and notes out. Now that's White_____.

The System (Of Oppression)

It's not just the black people who have a toxic and abusive relationship with the USA. It's any human being who operates by a system of oppression, for the oppressor is suffering just like the oppressed. Yes, it may seem like black people are suffering more and I think I agree with that ethos of thought, but the reality is the human race suffers in circumstances that lack equity. I believe we must always search for the root of problems with truth, not manipulated facts that aim to alter history and the course of humanity. Information is power and many will aspire to control the media and how people are cultured. Forgiveness and compassion are necessities to foster hope. We have to aim for peace, because that is why we are here.

Have you ever had an insect on your body or had an ant start to crawl down your arm? Well, we are the ants on the arms of Earth and the body is spinning faster trying to shake us off. If we don't get our shit right ASAP, we will evaporate, because earth mirrors us and we mirror earth. The planet wants peace, but only we can only have it if we find the right road.

Our parents were raised in a different era. There were consistent trials and errors, because that's life. The previous generations operated from a place /collective zeitgeist of limited information. They knew what they knew and now know what they know. While raising their children they did the best they could. We've been blessed with increased access to information and wisdom that positions us to better help our parents heal. And as we help them heal we indirectly and directly heal ourselves as well. Our parents only know what they know and for Luckily, for those of us gifted in principles around psycho education and therapy we can see that our self esteem, abandonment, rejection and self hate issues, stem from our parents. In this position it is our duty to help them find peace and wholeness as they step deeper into their legacy.

(Fixing) The System

America was founded on violence, conflict and bloodshed. It was not founded in healing practices and is karmically designed to repeat a cycle that can only be broken by self development leading towards an internal river of love.

We are born into a broken world with broken systems in which we internalize brokenness through socialization in our households and communities. Many of us spend much of our lives absorbing earthly ways only to unearth the pieces of our authentic selves. Only the courageous will be able to complete this walk. It includes getting raw, real, and fully invested in the truth of your source and self. Your good, bad and ugly have to be surfaced after being submerged for so long, so you can explore how you've arrived at the present. This is the gift. This is the story, the journey, the thread of experiences that made you who you've become.

Since I was in college I wanted to be an inspirational and transformative speaker that could change lives. I also felt drawn to healing. In a society that only values healing after blood is spilled it is mighty hard to reach.

And God said, "that's what you want! Ok. Here ya go" and all hell broke loose from within. It also broke away from the outside as well.

They say when you're getting married you are leveling up. And in leveling up, you will leave some things behind. You will leave some people behind, but most importantly you will leave the old you behind.

You will shed.

You will be transformed forever. God is drowning you, submerging you in the pool of yourself. Not for 9 months this time around, but longer.

It's been almost 1.5 years since I've been swimming by myself. In the submerging I'm seeing the many selves within. I'm seeing the different versions of Greg. It's the 4 year old, 8 year old, 15 year old, 21 year old, 30 year old and 39 year old Greg. The world has supported the fracturing of my many selves in order to blur my clarity of self and now I've been gifted with an opportunity to remember the many members within and bring them together as one. God has stretched me into pieces so I could remember who I was meant to be and not what the world made me. In becoming whole I am finding peace from the pieces of self and that alone is priceless.

I'm being reborn again.

The Planetary System: Oxygen For Sale

"It would be sad to achieve equity and freedom for more people and there not be a planet to enjoy it on."

\- @GregCorbinSpeaks

In 15 years Canada will be one of the most desired places to live. A while back it actually reached 100 degrees in Maine. This hasn't happened much in the past. It's practically unheard of in the past. Due to climate change, there is the possibility that the day will come when all land closest to the North Pole will be prime real estate. If you think gentrified inner cities have been changing. Wait until it's too hot to live in certain places.

"Oxygen for sale. Fresh air in a bottle. Oxygen tanks for the rich and wealthy."

\- @GregCorbinSpeaks

The planet is warming the same way a body will when it's infected. The body is magical. It will create an environment to get rid of the illness or disease in order to ease its anatomy. Humans have done more damage to the body of the planet in the last 150 years than in the previous 500,000 years. Imagine some places experiencing Summer all year round, and not a gentle Summer. A Summer with global warming attributes, such as air pollution from oil refineries making oxygen a priceless commodity sold in stores. Signs will say, "Oxygen for sale", "Fresh air in a bottle", "Oxygen tanks for the rich and wealthy".

Therefore I'm dedicating more time to my Science background and (my Biology degree with years of experience teaching science in classrooms) and sharing the knowledge with whoever wants it.

It will be sad to achieve equity and freedom for more people and there not be a planet to enjoy.

PS - Just thinking about my children's children's children.

How about you?

#ClimateChange #GlobalWarming

My System: Mental Health

There's been an unsettling feeling within since Thursday's therapy session. The conversation has shifted to focusing on little Greg who's been angry and enraged at his father for a while. I'm struggling with helping myself. I know I need to focus on myself. Like, I need to ramp up self focus, because my escape is helping others gain what I actually need, so it seems like I'm being healed by helping others. But I'm not healing because this type of voyeuristic and vicarious healing may fill the wounds within, but is only temporary. How do I permanently heal? I've noticed in the last few days I've felt needy and in search of affirmation, driving myself to a higher standard with my work in fear that I may be doing something wrong. I am timidly moving internally when it comes to things I love like public speaking and teaching. I'm unorganized and unfocused, fighting for confidence. The more I'm focused outside of me, the more I'm neglecting myself. I'm thankful that I'm beginning to recognize these signs, so that's a huge blessing, because I'm finally understanding the way I'm wired.

I've noticed in my adult years that I love helping others, providing advice, inspiring and empowering people, because I desire to see them succeed. I'm great at creating spaces of intimacy and safety, spending time supporting other people's dreams. I've noticed that these are the things I also didn't receive consistently from my parents. There were moments when I didn't get the hug, the intimate words of affirmation, positive feedback, the safe space for open communication or that inspiring message to get me over the top.. It was a very masculine household where feminine softness and nurturing was missing. I was cultivated in an off balanced and off centered house where the energy vacillated. I needed nurturing and still I seek nurturing, which means I have to talk to my mother more, who struggled with providing nurturing for me. In hindsight, I understand it. But in young Greg's eyes I loathe and hold remorse for the upbringing and the lack of skills my mother and father had raising children. They did the best they could with what they knew.

Their environment and era of time lacked many things. My environment was very hardened with a blanket of fear and desperation that was connected to violence and death. Traumatic parenting reaches deep, because if parents are not aware of the trauma, then they internalize it, passing it on to their children.

Did my parents hold me enough? Were they working too hard to provide those needs? Did they create space for me to say no and honor my authentic voice?

What does healthy nurturing look like? What exactly was it that I needed when I was being cultivated in my home? What are some moments where those needs weren't met, that could have damaged my development?

(F) The System

Why Do They Loot?! Heard so many privileged people say it was stupid and outrageous.

It is non productive in so many ways. But the metaphor is loud and clear.

Tear down something when you can't tear down the system that is tearing you apart.

Anger.

Rage.

Desperation.

Trauma.

Injustice.

It's a gumbo of liquid dynamite waiting to ignite.

"My son cries when police get close to us because he thinks I'm going to end up dead." -Naim White

While we the people await the Ferguson verdict! There hasn't been anything said about the Walmart shooting in which JohnCrawford was gunned down by police who received a phone call about "a black man waving and pointing a gun at people."

The officer was not charged but when you watch the video you see something completely different as he talks on the phone in an aisle of BB guns. One which he was holding.

Mind you this happened about 6 days before Ferguson. There should be something done.

Words become flesh. The call said one thing and the SWAT team reacted it to it. No warning; just shot him down. No charges were filed on the police. He unfortunately died while his father was on the other side of the phone call. He heard his son's last breath. We only have but so many eyes for attention and emotional endurance of the spirit. When the story first broke the news made it seem like he was a crazy man waving a gun in the store. This case will be swept under the rug like so many that never get the attention because they never break to the news.

The stereotypes attached to Blackness and Black Men definitely feed this event. The collective subconscious and conscious paranoia is rarely discussed especially when the trauma becomes the reason why so many act out. It's deep when you hear so many young men mention "I'm not going to make it to 21. Why should I do the schoolwork or even go" or "My sister was crying because she's afraid that I will be killed like them" or "My son cries when police get close to us because he thinks I'm going to end up dead." All trauma. All disturbing. This has become the norm in certain communities. How do we heal and solve these issues? How do we build awareness around these problems? How do we maintain and address the mental health issues that come along with these events? We have work to do.

A New System

"Forget your perfect offering. There is a crack in everything; that's how the light gets in."-- Leonard Cohen 8

Alfred a 63 year-old man lighting candles after a blackout during an earthquake:

The system.
We don't need to fix the system.
We need a new system.
It's broken and it's breaking the people.
Breaking the people apart.
Dividing and conquering them constantly building separation with every pen-stroke on another bill or contract.
Every signature seems to part the people like the Red Sea.
And the blood is on the hands of those who sign these documents.
It's a system that's breaking people and leaving them broken. The system is so ill and sick that it makes money and builds an industry that feeds off of the brokenness of the people.
Who will fix the system?
Who will fix the people?
Who will make them whole again?
Who?
When?
Each person becomes a commodity in this system. Each crack in the body is how the light gets in, but the light is still dim.
There's an malignant illness where the country creates an economy around the broken.

The system is not broken.

It's working for someone.   It's working for someone.

It's working for someone.   It's working for someone.

Dammit!!!!

I'm so tired and sick from this sickness called Liberty.

Are you really free??!

Prisons.
Obesity.
Homelessness.
The Uneducated.
Racism.
And someone is making their life off of the broken.

Because there's money in fixing it, but only temporarily
because if you solve the problem you may not have any economy
left.

And there's no money in solutions,
just the problem.

"I need a light."

"Aye Ralphie. Get me my matches from the bannister downstairs."

Affirmations 2

In a world that is burning people out because

the *operating system*

is built on speed and fear,

please remember **YOU** are **A HUMAN BEING**

who needs
Z
      Z
            Z

      Z
Z
rest...

GET CENTERED. BURN SOME SAGE. CLEANSE YOUR SPACE. BE KIND AND ENJOY YOUR LIFE.

@GregCorbinSpeaks

(BUY THE T-SHIRT)

Healing

Joy Factory

Some people need their pain.

At times it's the only way people can experience joy. I know firsthand. Our ability to constantly overcome our pain, brings a sense of accomplishment. It also brings a cycle of addiction, because those who crave joy, but need pain will struggle when joy comes. Joy is a derivative from being at peace with your present state internally as well as externally, but if people need pain to thrive and succeed, then people will search for relationships, scenarios, dynamics, and situations that will grant them the wish of conflict.

"SOME PEOPLE WHO ARE ADDICTED TO PAIN, THEY WILL CREATE THE ENVIRONMENT FOR CONFLICT AND DRAMA, BECAUSE DEEP INSIDE THEIR CORE BELIEF IS THEY NEED PAIN IN ORDER TO EXPERIENCE JOY."
- @GregCorbinSpeaks

And if you need pain and conflict to bring about joy, then your peace which brings joy will only last as long as you can stay in withdrawal from the addiction to pain. People who are addicted to pain, will create the environment for conflict and drama, because deep inside their core belief is they need pain in order to experience joy. Their identity is constructed to create chaos, because peace is too frightening. When order settles in they will disrupt it until they create their comfort zone or their joy factory where the rotating gears reside.

Some people want their pain.

Surrender

"Something amazing happens when we surrender and just love. We melt into another world, a realm of power already within us. The world changes when we change. the world softens when we soften. The world loves us when we choose to love the world." - **Marianne Williamson** 9

In order for you to step into the best version of yourself, you must release some dead things. We spend years building a mirage of identity fighting to make it a part of life, when in reality the identity is an illusion that we are making real. It's an attachment, latching onto the core, sending conflicting messages with the most genuine parts of who we really are. Eventually the confusion causes enough chaos, whereas the only way we can find order is to melt away those parts that take our breath away in a fire of brave space intentions. **In order to breathe deeply with clarity, we must disrupt fear at its core, shattering the trepidation of anxiety anchoring in our heart, beating a drum of a warrior song.**

To sing, we must endure, remain consistent, travel a road into our mind and heart. It's gonna hurt like hell, like a migraine wrestling a wisdom tooth in the middle of puberty, but it's gonna bring you the heaven you deserve.

the dead things: habits
      the dead things: patterns
           the dead things: victim stories
                the dead things: some people

Yes it's uncomfortable, heart twisting, and gut wrenching, but it's worth every step.

There's nothing more powerful than grieving the old you, mourning over the shadow self, and transforming into the person the world needs you to be, and not who people need you to be.

This is so damn liberating!

Sing that song.
Sing.
Sing.
Sing.

Ego Death

Dear _____

You must avoid being engaged and trapped in your fear of abandonment. Behaving from this point of view will cause you to make decisions based on company and not individuality. Your fear of isolation will cause you to compromise your integrity and true identity. Be aware when childhood traumas and experiences make special appearances as your "inner child" and influence dictation of your decision making process.

"HOW MANY TRUTHS CAN CO-EXIST IN THE SAME ROOM SIMULTANEOUSLY?" - @GregCorbinSpeaks

Do make decisions from a place of peace and understanding that all people and inhabitants of the earth plane will not be aligned with your way of thinking, your perspective, line of behavior and/or rules of engagement/ agreements.

Do create a space of love within so strong that is unbreakable and indestructible. An energy source that is centered on your personal boundaries and agreements with the earth plane that bring you joy, peace, gratitude and love. It is imperative for you to remember at times humans will blindly interact from their perspectives and personal interest, therefore some will feel betrayed when their ideas, perspectives, and attitudes conflict with yours.

How many truths can co-exist in the same room simultaneously? You have to allow belief systems and deeply entrenched habits that are locked into your body to be released, but first you must

172

become "aware" of your attachment(s). When you grow total consciousness of your mind-body connection, you can identify what emotions cause certain reactions in your being.

This is challenging, because you must come to grips with the fact that you are addicted to certain energies that manifest in the form of attitudes, thoughts, and behaviors. This generated energy is usually dictated by the ego when fear is the motivation. Your needle is the addiction via emotion that is hardwired into your body since childhood. You are fighting your own body, your own mind and the battle is for your spirit. The mind must master the workings of the programmed flesh mentality in order to fully experience liberation. You must learn to be in the world and not of it.

Speak Your Peace: On Fighting Perfectionism

By not speaking your true voice, you're ignoring your authenticity, and the opportunity to practice fair and equitable exchanges with people. Your fear of making mistakes (the overall feeling of being trouble) prevents you from being resilient, because you don't want to feel like a disappointment. So you rely on people pleasing instead of pleasing yourself, making yourself feel good about being you. You rely on making everyone happy first instead of acting, behaving and engaging from a space that pleases you. Your fear of conflict is deeply connected to not wanting to let people down. You're going to have to start engaging with life from a space that honors your true voice, divine form, and purposeful destiny.

How do you handle failure and adversity?

"I Like Me".

"I Love Me".

Use these affirmations to amplify the truth of who you can and will be. You're the one holding you back. You're the one muting your voice. You're the one falling into fear and not faith. You're the one inner communicating negative thoughts to you. You're the one creating scenarios where your voice isn't valuable.

No one else is doing this to you. You hit a wall literally because you got tired of your voice hitting you internally. It's only so much you can hold back. It's the worst betrayal. The one where you forget how powerful God made you. God made you electrically powerful, beautifully vulnerable, balanced, and imperfect.

This is a point of reflection your ongoing conflict is internal. ████████ has no clue how you feel and how she's showing up in your life. She is here for your growth. Where is it that you need to grow? What is it that you're supposed to learn? This feeling is not anxiety, it's actually you expanding and evolving. Your fears will consistently come up and show themselves to you. What is it that you need to do to be free of your old pattern and what does your inner child need to experience and hear from you in order to free himself ?

Remember there is a generational gap at play that is in play and you must work toward bridging the gaps with patience, humility, and love, yet still being firm enough to stand your ground and truth when necessary. You must find a balance between your present moment and your visionary gift. You have to work on being present in those meetings and remembering the main goal which is an objective learning experience where youth have an opportunity to practice real world dynamics and experiences that showcase moments of growth and discovery to themselves and one another. It is a place where the acts of love (forgiveness, redemption, grace, patience, empathy) live openly. Yes it's a challenge, but this is the saving grace of the world. There are many forms of justice, yet restorative and healing justice are not focused on enough. Yes systems are key, but are we creating balance in the discussion to involve healthy coping mechanisms and healing modalities?

We've enlightened them about systems and things that cause trauma, but we haven't really delved deeper into restorative principles which is high key and will be necessary in their organizing and campaign development.

On Sports And Joel Embiid

Courting Emotion

I have much respect to #JoelEmbiid for not letting unhealthy masculinity practices get in the way of him shedding tears. Here's why it was important for Joel Embiid to cry. Tears, the agony of defeat and so much more. It was such a stunning moment. The ball literally bounced four times before falling through the cylinder, capping off the amazing performance by offensive juggernaut Kawhi Leonard. I haven't seen any player that consistent and unstoppable during a playoff series.

Another thing that was refreshing was the tears streaming down Joel Embiid's face after the shot was launched 18.5 feet into the air over his outstretched hand. I haven't witnessed a player become so overwhelmed with emotion that he would break down on the opposing teams shoulders. Many know Joel Embiid as the fun loving fan favorite, and quick to clap back on social media all star Center. He reminded many people that human's cry when disappointed. When we lose something. When we are grieving that things didn't go as exactly planned.

I recently facilitated a workshop on emotional intelligence for a room of 80 plus men. As momentum picks up with men's healing and destigmatizing mental health, it is important we see it in such a public sphere. We all have the capacity to cry, but many people do not. Some learn to internalize their emotion, which transforms into chronic illnesses, outbursts, violence, addiction and displacement. Emotion is energy in motion and if that emotion is not released it becomes trapped in the body and harbors in the cells. Those cells have something called cellular memory. In other words, the body doesn't forget what it hasn't dealt with. Much of the disease we manifest as human beings comes from withholding stress, which causes 90% of strokes.

I recall a short documentary I did a while back on Black Male Vulnerability in which someone mentioned, "If you were crying, parents would send you upstairs to cry alone, 'You crying!? Go upstairs and cry!' "

When boys are taught to cry alone they learn to hide their emotions, devalue their emotions and perceive their emotions not just as a weakness, but an action that could earn separation and abandonment. Many men have abandonment issues and separation anxiety that will manifest in certain attitudes, behaviors and word choices. Black Men have been dehumanized, persecuted, conditioned in environments where hyper vigilance is embedded into our subconscious. Of course toxic masculinity would manifest when you are being cultivated in toxic environments in which internalized trauma and oppression is the norm. When your only focus is survival, it is hard to reflect, learn and grow holistically. I am thankful for the tears and humility of Joel Embiid this past weekend. More of that vulnerability is needed.

I CRY! I CRY and yes I CRY. I am a human first. Man second. At times it's the 7 year old who was told to stand in the corner crying through me. At times it's the 15 year old who was afraid to tell his parents that he was failing classes crying through me. At times it's the 27 year old going through a breakup crying through me. The more I cry the more healing occurs. I know the power of emotional repression and will not allow that to beat me again. Through these writings I've been able to inspire at least 15 other men to visit a therapist's office. I'm so proud of this.

On Sports And A Man Named UTE.

I was playing football in the snow. It was 7 on 7. My hands were freezing. My feet dressed in two pairs of socks to insulate the heat. We were young and wild playing under clouds, gliding in tough tundra trying to enjoy the day off from school. One name. UTE. He was built like a grown man and only 3 years older than me. Someone threw a screen pass to me. I caught it. Probably the dumbest catch ever. At this point in my teenage years I was searching for identity and a sense of belonging. I desperately wanted to prove I was tough and could handle physical conflict. Even if the game was such a violent game of harm and competition like football. It's kind of stupid that we didn't have helmets on while playing. No pads. We were reckless, but it was so fun. This was my blue collar athletic way of proving I was a man. Well at least becoming one. Well had the ball in my hands. UTE ran at full speed. 230 pounds of muscle. How'd I know that? I asked him the next day. 230 pounds of muscle hauling at me at hyper speed. I froze.

Now at this moment. You know I messed up. All I had to do was sidestep, move right or left before he tackled me like a Mac Truck hitting a deer. I flew back at least 5 yards. He landed on top of me like an animal that just caught his prey. Truth be told, I wanted to see if I could take the hit. I wanted to prove to myself I was tough enough to survive such an event. And It was quite an event for a 14 year old. I fed into the masculine stereotype that a man should be able to take pain and endure physical conflict. That I had to face it head on. That using my brain to move out the way of trouble was out of the question. Well, UTE knocked the wind out of me.

I got up with snow on my face. It was in my hair. Yeah. No helmet. No skull hat. Just fun. Just reckless fun. I took a hit to prove I was man enough. I took a hit because my intelligence wouldn't get me the street Cred and acceptance I needed for esteem. For confidence. I didn't just take a hit to prove I was a man or man enough. I did it to gain friendship. To gain a memory. To acquire a story to share. My intentions were not as confident as I would then like to be, but I was growing and learning. UTE trucked me as we would say. And I got up.

I don't play football anymore. I thought I would be one of those guys. Then I realized getting hit when you're older may not be smart. It would probably be painful. UTE!

Mirror Work

I want you to look deep into *your* eyes.

When's the last time you celebrated yourself?

Do you downplay your success?

Do you micromanage your greatness?

Do you play small because it's comfortable and comes with less pressure?

You don't deserve silence, you deserve greatness. I've certainly done this from time to time. I've downplayed my greatness and dimmed my light. All because I was concerned that it would make others uncomfortable. I'm not sure if it's fear or my ability to go weeks on burn out and still get things accomplished. The sad part about accomplishing goals while burnt out is that you struggle to accept the success, and celebrate the moment. The addiction to working and being active can make an individual feel like the accomplishment isn't good enough, which registers the accomplishment as invaluable. This causes a sense of resentment for the work that has been applied.

Self care is an unbelievable teacher. It's a classroom full of regrets, anxiety attacks, breakdowns, and unpredictable tears white water rafting down your face, while the bags develop under your eyes. But no one really understands what's in those bags. The ambitious hunger for success? A deep seeded yearning to accomplish your goals and maximize the ideas?

It's a struggle that can push us into not caring for our own well being. A place in mind where we begin to dictate our own lives based on a definition of success that's not of our own, but of our environments. We grind. Yes we work hard. By all means we aim to accomplish.

180

Sometimes it's a calling.
Sometimes it's about the acceptance of others.
No matter what the motivator and intention may be.

WE MUST REMEMBER TO

stretch
breathe
drink water
eat healthy
breathe
pray
meditate
sleep

Without allowing the grind
to grind us into pieces of peace
that become chaotic dream chasers
dancing in our mind and spirit.
The grind can destroy us if not handled right.

In some cases many have become addicts of worry focused on being left behind, desperate locked in competition with everyone except ourselves. Using our egos and not enough spirit to push through the task. Although we need ego, we need spirit more.

We need faith even more. You don't have to destroy others dreams or successes to make your own creations better. Your ideas are already great because they come from a place of divinity. Burning out while grinding yourself into the ground is the fastest way to self-destruct, and become dust, only to be blown away by the vigorous movement of life.

Dream Weaving: Creating Your Own Reality

One of the best accomplishments a person can achieve is discovering the truest version of who they were destined to be. In that moment lives the purpose of why you were born. Each talent and gift you've been provided appears crystal clear for you to observe, interview and fearlessly apply. This doesn't mean curiosity is no longer necessary. It's actually more important as you move through this journey of life.

For years we operate from a program that is installed in our first seven years of life, when the subconscious mind is mostly present, in which we develop implicit memories or automatic memories. Our eyes serve as cameras, recording each interaction between people, places and things, and then downloading the information into our subconscious and conscious mind. Our primary caretakers in households, school settings, religious sanctuaries, and the outside world indoctrinate us with a set of beliefs and norms that we barely question. Is this your reality? Is this your imagination?

"If we aren't in control of the things that bring us sustenance and survivability, how do we gain a sense of true independence?"
- @GregCorbinSpeaks

At our birth our minds are clean slates waiting for information. For generations people in certain societies have been conditioned to give away their choice, limiting their power, sovereignty, and autonomy over their lives making them codependent individuals who depend on systems provided by the government. It took me years to truly understand how much I wasn't in control of where my food came from, where my clothes were created, and how to build shelter.

We depend on a grid of supply chains to import resources that help us meet our basic needs, without truly exploring what it looks like when the chain is untethered. If we aren't in control of the things that bring us sustenance and survivability, how do we gain a sense of true independence? As long as we depend on the system to deliver resources that meet our basic needs we have to think deeply if that is true freedom.

As an educator, I know firsthand there should be a class on systems, logistics, and geography in elementary that will help expand the mentality and imagination of students. If done right, it can amplify the capacity of their learning and problem solving ability. For example, let us examine the American school learning experience. Monday through Friday, students attend school for eight hours a day, five days a week over a stretch of 12 years to graduate with a diploma. Over a 12 year span you study external information, learning about the workings of the world, but simultaneously neglecting the inner workings of yourself.

"You do have power to think outside of the box by sitting in stillness for reflection and restoration. When this is done you create more room and opportunity to hear your inner voice. Your inner voice is an asset that is supported by another asset, time."
- @GregCorbinSpeaks

We learn how to consume information in order to be workers for the national economy that is in competition with a global economy, falling in love with optional jobs that are inherited from previous generations. Previous generations that were indoctrinated to find meaning in what jobs the industrial revolution provided, along with entrepreneurial ventures that would emerge. We come to discover that we have committed ourselves to an asylum of delusional sanity that mirrors itself as insanity, but this discovery only occurs when you reject the world inside your mind, which isn't even your world. It's someone else's, but you do have power.

You do have power to think outside of the box by sitting in stillness for reflection and restoration. When this is done you create more room and opportunity to hear your inner voice. Your inner voice is an asset that is supported by another asset, time. Time is the most valuable asset an individual has. Where we spend it is a reflection of our values. Furthermore it is an investment, and many of us never put down our indoctrination and conditioning long enough to invest in ourselves. To study ourselves. To witness our patterns. Through indoctrination your imagination is given a box, a set of parameters. A limited paradigm. A set of beliefs and values you've inherited are in control of your decisions, and also your expectations. **In a world of make believe, those who control the beliefs, control expectation. Those who control expectations control imagination. Imagination is your superpower, but only if you're willing to do the work.** This is your opportunity to create your reality. Go inward.

"Maybe you aren't breaking down, but finally breaking open, so that you can break through?"
- @GregCorbinSpeaks

And when we do sit still we may discover that we are in constant performance, performing identity markers such as race, class, gender, religion and more. It's all a show on a stage called life. All social constructs created from the imagination of another person that came before us. **It's all in your mind.** Each identity is heavy with expectation, simultaneously creating opportunity for internal and external conflict. They are jackets that we take from a closet of persona and drape them over our shoulders for use when necessary. There are times where the weight is too much for us to bear, causing midlife breakdowns.

Maybe you aren't breaking down, but finally breaking open, so that you can break through?

Maybe you are releasing the scripts and the stories that are no longer serving your highest good?

Maybe the practice of releasing bags of indoctrination life has provided you is how you grow lighter?

Maybe that's the purpose of life?
What would the world be without conflict?

Maybe that's why we come to this planet, this dimension where we forget that we are spiritual beings having a human experience. We journey through an environment of confusion in search of clarity, so that we can return back to ourselves whole. In that wholeness we find peace. We find healing and in our brightest hopes we find the truest version of who we are destined to be and become.

And maybe that is the best accomplishment.

Outgrowing the older versions of who we once were.

Far From a Fairy Tale

Dedicated to all the Activists

Once upon a time there was no happy ending. No princesses, princes, kings or queens.

There lived an activist who was passionate about their community. They volunteered their heart and soul.

> Their time and
> determination.
> One of the truly great.
> Offering tremendous
> soul work.

They began coming up short, making mistakes, because after all they were human. Their reputation was taking a hit. They began to show up late to meetings, missed organizing actions, and something was up.

> Their name would be
> dragged through the
> mud, sullied by
> uncompassionate acts.

A silent boycott of their gifts, talents, and ideas emerged, rippling throughout the community.

People began to ask about them.
Wondering about what would happen to them.
They had been suffering. Suffering from depression.
A long battle.
Won or lost?
One day they committed suicide.
No one checked in on them to see if they were ok. If they needed help?
If they needed a listening ear?

The burnout was real. The mental health and emotional wellness was real. The need to ask for help was real.

May we grow more compassionate for each other
as we walk forward in life.
People are pouring their heart, soul, mind, time
into many different movements
that advocate for other people than themselves.
May we remember that we are all human.
That we all need check in's.

We beat on one another like the system hasn't been designed
to produce suffering and transform it into profit.

We beat on one another with shame, judgement,
quick to dispose of one another like we don't have a lot in common.

We make decisions with ego and fear and not love and compassion. This isn't just a test about getting free. It's about forgiveness, communication, authenticity, honesty, truth and learning how to communicate it all with love.

Because that is the same love that will inspire someone
to be put on the front lines and back rooms with you.

People have opinions about people they don't even know. Learn how to connect and build meaningful relationships because we all have something to offer. This message is for the teachers/ the artists. Everyone. We all need each other. (This isn't a call to arms, but a call for arms. A call for arms to embrace each other- with love)

Share if you feel the need.

Affirmations 3: Be Love.

Become love in spite of all the devilish things that try to rip you to shreds. **See God in others as you wish to see God inside yourself.** That's when you will discover the truest form of love. A world without grace, redemption, forgiveness, patience is a world without love. To be honest a world without acts of love is a dangerous place. That's not a world I'm interested in building. I want no parts of that energy. No one is disposable or irredeemable. We often are quick to cancel and dispose of others because they remind us of who we are when we don't like ourselves and when we don't get it right. They remind us of the parts of self we haven't learned to heal and love yet. We ignore the backstory and how people arrive at destinations throughout their journey of living life. We dismantle our natural ability to practice compassion and empathy.

And yes I struggle, I'm not perfect by any means. Sometimes I get it right and sometimes I get it wrong. I'm human and I'm always here with a listening ear. I love phone conversation and not text because dialogue is a beautiful and valuable art form that may be dying. I cried with a friend on the phone last night. Just sobbing. And they responded with "you are loved". That doesn't make me weak, it actually makes me strong. Being vulnerable and not feeling threatened or afraid of being punished for it in some way was so healthy for me. We need more safe spaces. We need more healthy conversations that aren't laced with agendas and ego. I'm a being of love and that's what I choose to spread. Choice allows me to not play the game of life with a victim mindset. I do have control and as long as I take responsibility by being accountable to learning and growing through my experiences, then I've given myself the opportunity to transform to a better version of myself.

So for all those people out there being hard on yourself, let it go and move forward. You get another crack at doing it today. God isn't finished with you yet. You've got work to do. You serve a purpose. You serve God or however you see the Most High. Not people. People are finicky and selective. How do I know? Because I can be that way as well. I'm working on this as well. Activists can be some of the judgiest people. How do I know? Because I'm one of them as well. I'm working on that too, because none of us are perfect. People want truth and transparency but ain't ready to be truthful and transparent with themselves. All of us got some skeletons in the closet. I'm just getting more comfortable with my own. And one day soon I will share some in hopes to inspire and encourage others to keep pressing towards the mark.

I'm choosing love everyday. I'm truly becoming more excited about what God has in store for me next. And yes, it's beautiful. ❤

MAKE
LOVE
GREAT
AGAIN.
- @GregCorbinSpeaks

(BUY THE T-SHIRT)

Poems And Prose Interlude 2

20/20

In hindsight, I was a poet, trailblazing educator and visionary that identified a niche market of philanthropic service, helping the much needed, yet oppressed voice of youth. I spent thousands on a vision that many doubted, laughed in my face about, constantly ignored me, but something spiritual pushed me to keep going.

In hindsight I was a hard working, barely sleeping, over working perfectionist, who lacked business savvy, and operational skill sets. I felt guilty when I had to withhold information for the sake of professionalism, because it felt dishonest and disloyal, when in reality it went with a job description that I struggled to absorb. It went against the grain of what came easy to me.

"I was using master's tools to build a house of liberation. The more I focused on building, the more I built a prison for myself." - @GregCorbinSpeaks

In hindsight the internalized colonialism and oppression coursed through my being. I say this now in an era that is recognizing the impact of colonialism, which isn't taught with the full scope in school classrooms. There were some things I did that caused harm, replicated oppression. I was using master's tools to build a house of liberation. The more I focused on building, the more I built a prison for myself.

In hindsight, I wish those who place judgement on leadership without experience, please understand you will never have a clear picture or perspective of comprehension, because you have not walked the walk. And trust, you may not want to. I was blessed to build a dream into a reality, and will be building more as the future evolves. I'm beginning to release regret to absorb the wisdom. It took some time to see that the betrayal I experienced was all about my own decisions, although betrayal did occur, it is becoming more valuable.

"As executives and professionals we are conditioned, incentivized to move more like the system than the people and unfortunately many of us in leadership will never see it."
- @GregCorbinSpeaks

In hindsight, there's so much I would love to be publicly open about, but the concern of retaliation, digital attacks, induced shaming as if accountability is punitive halts that decision. A healthy form of accountability is intentionally restorative. It involves sitting with people to have courageous conversations in the name of love and not fear. It is about holding up the strengths and gifts of all while working towards an amplified awareness of how we can all do better.

"A healthy form of accountability is intentionally restorative. It involves sitting with people to have courageous conversations in the name of love and not fear." - @GregCorbinSpeaks

Not just those who do harm, but all. After all, life is a class and we all serve as lessons for one another. Those lessons can impact more if our mistakes weren't used against those who misstep, but were instead used in a more knowledgeable way to educate and empower. As executives and professionals we are conditioned, incentivized to move more like the system than the people and unfortunately many of us in leadership will never see it. We need to be more human, comprehensive, purposely intergenerational bridge builders with more than short term internships and apprenticeships. We need to create jobs for the generations that will one day replace us in these positions. They need opportunities, enhanced job creation that honors the world they come from. That is a world built on digital spaces, innovative models that inspire closeness. If we don't create space to understand each other, and what we are all facing we will grow further divided, boxed into silos, small communities built in response to fear and not love, survival and not thriving, trauma and not healing.

"We need to be more human, comprehensive, purposely intergenerational bridge builders with more than short term internships and apprenticeships."

- @GregCorbinSpeaks

Prose and Consumers

You know, the consumerism we participate in this country is one bounded by fiscal greed, emotional lust, intertwined with shadow personalities that rage internally. Imagine if the darker sides of self showed up in the country simultaneously. A moment when our implosions and explosions interface.

We consume media and become doppelgängers of socialized images on television. We consume emotions, feeding on the drama, yearning for conflict, eating the pain as if sacrifice knew us personally.

"This country is founded on snatching land, water, and animals, while simultaneously using genocidal energy to control the territory, therefore it is not surprising that there is a big conversation in communities about taking space." - @GregCorbinSpeaks

We consume people, building transactional relationships, objectifying then based on their gifts and assets. Many of us in this country have been conditioned to feed and feed and feed, addicted to greed. Craving attention, ego based dilemmas that confront our morality and mortality. Is this a place to raise a child, to build families? Is this a location where structured chaos is a norm we deny, yet welcome blindly? Is this a place where time is money and money is time?

There's always a cost. With the embedded paranoia tethered into the societal and energetic foundation of our country, I wonder will that same energy haunt us into a metaphysical cannibalistic attitude that will turn everyone on each other and eventually on themselves. This country is founded on snatching land, water, and animals, while simultaneously using genocidal energy to control the territory, therefore it is not surprising that there is a big conversation in communities about taking space.

This is a response when hurt is not repaired. When healing isn't the focus to bring wholeness to a broken country which is built on brokenness and unfulfilled needs. If we have a clear blueprint to become what this country is made of, how do we find positive solutions that can confront and halt that trajectory? How do we heal a country built on pain, using lust and greed as an economy building mechanism all under a guise of fear? How do we heal the brokenness within and find ways to heal it in others or at least make others aware of what society needs ?

Feathers

"Your task is not to seek for love, but merely to seek and find all the barriers within yourself that you have built against it."— **Rumi**

There is an African Spiritual Practice called MAAT. In MAAT the belief is in order for a person's soul to transition into the afterlife, their heart must be lighter than a feather. Can you imagine your heart being weighed on a scale of justice to see if it is lighter than a feather? This would mean you have surrendered heavy emotions such as sadness, grief, depression and transformed them into lighter emotions of joy, glee, celebration and calm. That is light!

The heart knows what the heart knows.

It is recognition that your innerwork has been done. Yet, this is not easy, because the heart knows what the heart knows. It is the place where truth lives, and death comes to die. There is nothing like dying before your physical death. Nothing like shedding the old you, until you no longer are recognizable. Nothing like understanding that people will drink from you as long as they can feed on you. Nothing like watching the bitter resentment leave your spirit in the name of forgiveness, only to watch the pain resurface.

The heart knows what the heart knows.
- @GregCorbinSpeaks

It knows betrayal, deep dark secrets laced underneath traumatic events living in the underbelly of grief. There's a part of you that is fighting to not seek revenge, aiming to play the good side. Then there's another part that says I want blood. I want people to suffer. I want them to see how easy this shit isn't. I want hurt, and betrayal for them. The heart knows what the heart knows. It knows that is not you. That is not your heart. That is not lighter than a feather.

Forgive.
Forgive.
Forgive.
Yourself.

- @GregCorbinSpeaks

You can't do anything about the past. It is a mere reflection teasing you with each memory that you have refused to learn from. You can't focus on the peripheral environment. You can only focus on you and how you move forward.

What will you build? What will you do next? What does your new job look like? What does your family look like? What will they value?

Food Glorious

I will not be letting the shame of mistakes haunt me, for I am so much more greater than anything that I've done wrong. I will not be disposing my...*Krush Groove.*

One of my favorite scenes, *The Fat Boys* singing *All You Can Eat* about eating everything possible at a Sbarro for $2.99! Inspiring to say the least. Ponderosa. Glory hallelujah!

The buffet there was what I lived for when I was younger. It was the apex of celebration for my stomach which developed a personality of its own for attention to detail when it came to food. My eyes were in my stomach at times becoming bigger than needed. Greed.

I would eat 3 plates at least for these momentary celebrations whether it be birthdays, graduations or just some random family night out. Gluttony.

I would eat like there was no tomorrow. I loved food as a treat, coping mechanism, celebration of worth, statement of addiction, and escape. Each chew was a journey of ecstasy. A trip between space and taste. Dependency and distraction from all the things I didn't want to address like bullying, not liking myself, being afraid that I would never lose weight, the stretch marks on the side of my stomach, the girl that I crushed on but didn't want me, the girls I crushed on but were too afraid to say something, the rejection, not being athletic enough, the destructive nicknames, the clothes I liked but couldn't fit, etc.

The addiction that snatches power from control and promotes your taste buds to make decisions for you. Moments when you know you've had enough but you stay like an obedient soldier with gluttonous goals to outdo yourself. Moments when you wait for the 3rd and 4th round. The addiction to escape and run away from all the things I couldn't stand about the world as I saw it and affected me. Bobs Big Boys for the breakfast buffet.

Man I was in heaven! Glory.

Bacon. French Toast. Hash Browns. Scrapple. Eggs. Cheese Eggs. Pancakes. Sausage. Glory! Pork. Beef. Turkey.

Didn't matter, I was going to eat to satisfy my stomach. My eyes were moving between my stomach and my tongue. Back and forth they fluctuated. All you can eat. All you can sneak into your mother's purse or your book bag. The greed attached to knowing the bargain and the sheer convenience of take and eat whatever you want in a seemingly limitless environment was extremely overwhelming. So overwhelming that it became normal. The scarcity that there's never going to be enough so I mind as well get it now. The fear this opportunity may never come again, although it came many times.

You'll Say What You Say and I'll Say àṣẹ

There will always be monsters, vampires, and leeches, who need blood in the water to thrive, finding comfort in their own shortcomings. They will come in the form of fake friends, associates, and unfortunately, even family at times. But be in reflection that their battle of self is not yours. Do your best to not take it personal. Move forward in your light and drink from the waters of purpose and divinity.

The monsters and vampires, the half-live half-dead beings will carry a darkness that only behaves, engages and interacts from a space of fear. A fear that they are only valuable in causing conflict, drama that will drink you empty and leave you dry. I've learned this lesson the hard way, although at the time I didn't know many other ways to learn it.

Each time it happens, I'm reminded that the dark within them is the jealousy, envy, hatred that they want but can not have. They want what you embody, discovered by mining your greatness, and earned by taking on this beautiful challenge of life. It's energy and vibration. If your spirit ain't right we can feel it.

We used to talk about this a lot in martial arts class.

The warriors of light understand the thirst comes from within. Sad when you forget that you were born with everything you ever needed. Let the monsters and vampires, the drama wearing werewolves who carry burdens from birth, the misguided ones who need conflict to thrive figure out that they are suffering on their own.

We have no time to be distracted by ego and fear. May we move in forgiveness, be protected by divine intelligence to make choices that are healthy, and produce the best that God has to offer through our spirits, beings, flesh and bones.

Feel free to share. àṣẹ.*

*àṣẹ **(Ashe)** is an energy and divine force and power incarnate in the world. Olodumare gives **àṣẹ** to everything, including inanimate objects. àṣẹ is the power behind all things in the universe. It enables people to find balance in life.

Each

Each person is a word spoken by God.
Look at how the words treat one another.

Plan-demic

God has a plan.
She's just waiting for you to stop trying to enforce yours.

You Are Not

You are not your mistakes.
You are not your mistakes.
You are not your mistakes.
You are not your mistakes.
You are not your mistakes.
You are not your mistakes.
You are not your mistakes.
  - @GregCorbinSpeaks

Fragile Life

Life is fragile.
Be gentle with each other people.
Life is fragile.
Be gentle with each other people.
Life is fragile.
Be gentle with each other people.
Life is fragile.
Be gentle with each other people.
Life is fragile.
Be gentle with each other people.

- @GregCorbinSpeaks

Just Some Thoughts

My hands grasped an orange with 23 seeds in it, while 150 plus people stood in line for a video game.
*

Ever since first watching Star Wars as a young child, I've wondered about the merging of machines and humans. In my mind, the cyborgs have been coming for a long time. We will soon be in a world where robots (if not already) will walk the streets and humans will continue to integrate robot technology to supplement the things that may be missing. There are so many movies that have shown the coming of these days, which always prompts me to ask how much technology are they keeping behind closed doors and what does the strategic plan look like?
*

Every classroom should have the games:
Bananagrams and Taboo.
*

One improves vocabulary and comprehensive motor skills while the other expands quick witted critical thinking along with social awareness and context.

How are You?

"I'm fine" can be a dangerous statement when in reality some people are not fine, they are hurting. They could even be depressed struggling with self acceptance and self esteem. We are multilayered and multicultural people with many facets to our person.

Sometimes it is that simple. We are fine.

There are moments when we are not. The challenge is knowing when to own that, while having the courage to be vulnerable and reach out to our support system when you do not trust you are fine.

We all need help.

We all need help.

We all need help.

- @GregCorbinSpeaks

Trust I know. It's been a battle but I'm learning everyday how to ask for help when needed and how to accept that it takes a community of support to be one's best self.

LIKE THIS

Some are living for **likes** and not for what we love about ourselves.

Social media is a game of illusion. It is a powerful thing.

Some are living for **likes** and not for what we love about ourselves.

Unfortunately we live in a society where capitalism teaches people that we have to treat people like a commodity, making our exchanges transactional further objectifying our humanness. And making others steps and means to an end goal.

Some are living for **likes** and not for what we love about ourselves.

We must find a better way to check in with one another because human connection is a necessity. It is oxygen.

Some are living for **likes** and not for what we love about ourselves.

Intimacy is the superpower behind our vitality. Being able to express our full authentic person without ~~worry~~ for repercussion.

Some are living for **likes** and not for what we love about ourselves.

Rediscovering how to love, and the truest form of love which is giving without expecting anything in return.

Some are living for **likes** and not for what we love about ourselves.

We must give love to self first in order to give to others.

Some are living for **likes** and not for what we love about ourselves.
Transactional and consumer-based relationships drive a wedge between our relationships.

Some are living for **likes** and not for what we love about ourselves.

When we manage how we relate to one another based on expectations and what we will get out of it/them, we limit the infinite possibilities that are in store for these relationships.

8 Moments That Made Me Smile

1.
Teaching pre-teens how to critically think for themselves.
Not what the world spoon feeds them.
We shared a plate of knowledge.
Their courage and answers were amazing.
They showed the vulnerability you struggle to get from adults.

2.
Discovering how well some of my mentees can rap.
Like now they are really good.
Like really good.
They actually know each other's songs.
Poetry opens you up to so many possibilities.

3.
We ciphered, shared verses, mending generations of knowledge.
Using metaphor and simile to patchwork the wounds of
intergenerational trauma and disruption.
Elements we became, shifting the wind of tomorrow with flamed
shaped tongues.

4.
Witnessing Jamarr Hall connect with children who are from the
same projects that raised him.
He provided a different possibility for them.
His beacon of light shining like a compass of courage.
They found direction in his words.
Those exchanges are the ones that expand your world.

5.
(Five) Senses.
Being able to see.
Being able to taste.
Being able to feel.
Being able to smell.

Being able to walk and compose sentences.
Being able to hear each word exchanged.
I am thankful.

6.
Arriving home to build a house of clarity within.
A space for reflection in which to become sermon..
(In)side the (purpose) of the youth provided more (purpose)
The strength to ignore the remote control,
dismissing the media.
Understanding at times it's just too darn much.
If you feel beat down it's hard to help others up.

7.
Thinking about how dope TOP 5 MC debates can really be.
Today my top 5 is:
Kane
KRS- ONE
Rakim
Dre 3000
(Pos)dnous of De La Soul

8.
GOD

"To return to love, to get the love we always wanted but never had, to have the love we want but are not prepared to give, we seek romantic relationships. We believe these relationships, more than any other, will rescue and redeem us."

- From the always insightful *Bell Hooks; All About Love.*

The Letters of Love

83% of teenagers have not written a love letter.

They are missing out.

That's deep.

I remember writing love letters to girls I would never give them to. It's so terrifying putting yourself out there, vulnerable, patiently, yet anxiously waiting for an answer, as you wear your emotions on the sleeve.

I recall writing a love letter in my 20's and got rejected. Well it was kind of a "will you go out with me?" date letter.

I currently write my wife love letters, doing my best to celebrate love and surprise her with random moments of joy. All people need acceptance, approval and appreciation. I am learning each day the importance to court my wife at every turn of our marriage. We are constantly evolving. Growing together versus growing apart takes work, consistency, discipline and effective communication. Like any other relationship marriage is work and it only works if you work it.

Hence a working relationship.

We all just want to be loved.

Valued for being alive.

We want to matter.

Gratitude to all who have not been thanked for being awesome!

"True love does have the power to redeem, but only if we are ready for redemption. Love saves us only if we want to be saved."

- From the always insightful *Bell Hooks; All About Love.* 10

Some Call Control, Freedom!

I know a **man**, man with a

face shaped

like a ***bouquet*** of coffins.

His **smile** flowering with a tombstone tongue

speaking in an ***unknown*** language,

waiting for a deadly blooming.

Tomorrow he will pick the petals from a ***garden***

as **gorgeous** as the grey in his skin.

There is where he will find ***life***.

Open Letter 1

Dear Kaepernick
They only loved you for your body, not your mind.
We see them.

Open Letter 2

Dear Young People

Please do your best to not have children until you learn how to sustain yourself. Even if that means sustaining your livelihood with jobs you don't want to perform.

Sometimes you have to do the things you don't want to, to have the things you need.

I keep coming across young people; some are teenagers who aren't thinking with a long term perspective of life. The responsibility it takes to raise another human being into a productive and functional citizen.

Too many children are having children.
#TRUTH

(A Young) Brother

Last week a young brother told me, "I get high to numb the pain. No one wants to feel the life I'm living. You'd be paranoid, always watching your back, afraid the next person out to get you is riding by. I'm trying to forget this life. I just want to escape. Jump out of my skin. Leave this flesh and bone s**t behind, because I don't even want to be here sometimes. Would you want to live the way I'm living?"

And I responded,

"No, but you have a choice that doesn't depend on your past. You dictate your future. You draw the map to the gold. You are the treasure. Someone is making money off of everything you breathe, because you forgot your genius and brilliance. And you are brilliant and you are a genius, but no matter what I say, you have to believe in it! In you! That's why you're locked up. You have given away so much power that you just told me; you aren't even aware of the life you're living and when you are, you don't even want it. So you get high to forget it. If you don't like the life you're loving you have to change it. You have to inspire yourself from within. You have to make the choice. Ask how? Study! Ask for help! Use the people around you and ask!! Ask! Ask! You are someone's promise and you were not put here to be broken."

Open Letter(s) 3-6

Dear Men

It's ok to hurt.
It's ok to say you are hurting.
It is not a weakness to feel pain.
It is human.

Holding it in to explode and project onto others is destructive and dangerous. In the past few days it's been brought to my attention that three women were killed by the anger and rage of their boyfriends fueled by their ego and insecurity. It has been time for a shift in the way we see manhood and masculinity.

We need to teach healthier ways to deal with hurt to boys and men who learn these generational curses, disruptive myths and habits.

The time for healing is now.

I remember a woman telling me after a performance "I didn't know a man could feel that way. That a man could hurt and hurt for others. I thought it just didn't exist". She was 63 years old. It blew my mind, because for years she didn't even expect men to be fully functional human beings who were capable of feeling and emoting beyond the anger and aggression she was use to. We have to step it up. Especially us men.

"I wish we all knew how to grieve well, to be empowered by our tears, to be stable in the idea that we must cry and that weeping is part of the fight. Especially my little boys. My dear little boys who are parading as men, who miss their friends and are weeping without showing it."
- Chinaka Hodge

Dear Men

I dare you to say "I Love You" to another man today. We grow so afraid of one another that we have to relearn how to trust one another. Especially Black Men!

Lesson 1: Appreciate yourself. Be grateful for your consistent offerings to the community. Recognize that you are worthy like anyone else. People treat you the way you treat yourself, so be gracious and glorious with your energy, because you are needed even when you believe you are not. Trust, you are.

"Our soulmate is someone who shares our deepest longings, our sense of direction. When we're two balloons, and together our direction is up, chances are we've found the right person. Our soulmate is the one who makes life come to life." - Richard Bach 11

Dear America

Acid in the wound.
Blood in the lungs.
Bleach in the eyes.
#ericgarner

Dear Black Men

I've walked into stores and been followed multiple times since I was young. The perpetuated fear and stereotypes constantly living around me trying to break my energy field, destroy my aura while tearing down my self esteem. But I understand you want the light, the eternal filament that my wings carry. No matter how much you are taught to fear me you will always be proven wrong. You will always have to rethink why you ever devalued my/our character in the first place. It's not easy wearing a crown that others forgot you were born with. At a time when even your own have been taught to fear you. **You are not broken. You will always pick up the shattered shards and piece them back together.**

Peace them back together.

You will peace back together in a whole new way because you are healing and unconditionally loving, even when so many have been conditioned to hate you. You will always prove them wrong. So love anyway. Heal anyway. Ask the questions that will make you grow. Move past the past and enter a new world of thought.

Love is the way.
Whatever you do.
Do it with love in heart.
Make your intentions love.
We don't have to prove them wrong.
They will feel the shame of their prejudice.
We are beyond intelligent and the bottled generations of ignorance.

#blackmen
#men #healing
#healing #racism #hatred
#love #heart

Affirmations 4

Work on yourself.
Talk to yourself.
Focus on yourself.
Love yourself.
Think for yourself.

           Work on yourself.
           Talk to yourself.
           Focus on yourself.
           Love yourself.
           Think for yourself.

                      Work on yourself.
                      Talk to yourself.
                      Focus on yourself.
                      Love yourself.
                      Think for yourself.

Work on yourself.
Talk to yourself.
Focus on yourself.
Love yourself.
Think for yourself.

           Work on yourself.
           Talk to yourself.
           Focus on yourself.
           Love yourself.
           Think for yourself.

                      Work on yourself.
                      Talk to yourself.
                      Focus on yourself.
                      Love yourself.
                      Think for yourself.

And so on ....

JOY IS AN INSIDE JOB.

@GregCorbinSpeaks

(BUY THE T-SHIRT)

Final Interlude 3

To Give and Give-up

The easiest thing a person can do is give up on another human being. Sometimes we wait for other people to give us confidence with a decision, when in reality they are waiting for us to make a decision. You also have to pay attention to the noise, the articulate distractions. People trying to influence your world through their perspective. Some know how to do this with love and some don't. I have a knack for not giving up on people, but simultaneously not asking for help. That will change and all the doubt will too. Whether you like it or not it will change. So keep figuring out ways to not help rather than help. If you ain't helping me build, get out of my way. I mean it. Whether I verbalize or show it with my actions, you will get the message.

For(Give)ness

I forgive those with darkened hearts.
Those that forgot
they were born with light
and a laughter that could crack the clouds of rain open for the sun.
Those who speak a silent desperation, whispering from ear to ear
in hopes that their brewing storm can become the eye in a
hurricane of chaos.

I forgive you
for believing something built on the elements of love
could actually fall victim to the chaotic hatred you boil and spill on
your stove of greatness.

The only thing being prepped here, for a meal, is justice, peace, love
and kindness.

I have decided to love you gently
in hopes I remind you of who you really are
and who you really are meant to be.
Because every light

has a shadow.

Life And Death

The other night I witnessed Death knocking on the door of another person's life. A man bleeding from the head shortly after an accident died in a hospital. I am still processing this life and death thing. I'm gonna be darned if I let the stupidest things get under my skin. Life is too fragile and delicate. We forget. We are in love with ego. The ability to put people down when we are up. Stepping on the backs of others to elevate is a quick way to hang yourself. We are a community fighting to remember that we are all human and all learning. Radical love!

It never amazes me how people treat you when you don't agree with them. It's called being an individual.

Spiritual warfare is the first attack; but what happens when the people don't even notice that they are spirit first!?

They fight one another.

Old   AND   Young

I see the old grow old
because they choose
to grow old.

They disconnect themselves   from the ways
of the youth.
They choose not to understand   by not listening
to their voices.
The elders
must do better

         to listen to the
         youth.

         And the youth
         must do better.

     Communication
     Is a two way street.

         The young
        struggle

to listen to the older generations
bc older generations
have modeled the way.

         And the young
         don't pay
       attention

to what you say,
as much as they respond   to how you
act!

We all have to
do better listening.
It will change
our communities.

FEAR Affirmation 5

FEAR will not move me from my purpose.
It will not steal me of my gifts and talents.
Although it will show its face it will not remove me
of my maximum potential.

FEAR, your ways of worry, of being indecisive and of being
ashamed will not plague me into a corner of non-productivity.

F E A R will be transformed into **love and light**.

Into **energy** that is progressive and impactful.
There is no need to allow it to take over my life, but there is the
need to be aware of when it is stealing my power.

I have come so far and have much more of a journey to travel.
The peaks and valleys are all real and set to provide a classroom of
learning on this planet
as I interact with this world.

I'm in the process of changing the habits that are no longer
productive in my life.

Construction is an understatement.

This leadership institute has me looking at myself
in ways I have struggled to observe in myself for years.

I would like to thank every human in the world who has played a
role
whether it was good or not so good.

We are all here to help each other **GROW**.

Everything that I have done that has regressed or become stagnant
in some way

is related to my habits. The same goes for all the good and progressive things I have done. **HABITS**.

Your behavior is your character. It is your legacy. (Cues MJ's *Man in the Mirror*)

The **POWER** of your voice is an exceptional need.

It is   breath
when others choose to

        suffocate in silence.

When the heart is a tidal wave
      and pulls you under
           your worst fears.
                Keep swimming towards
                SURVIVAL.

Being aimless in life   with no real intention of leaving a mark

is a sad story to write.

Especially when you never knew the pencil was in your hand.

Not knowing your POTENTIALl or **POWER** is fast track failure with reprised repercussions.

In order to build a life you don't want to take a vacation from

you must embrace all the things you don't like doing.
No dream is perfect! It's all a blessing!

Many things go into dirt. But there's a difference in being planted and being buried.

"Are you a seed or a corpse?" - *Javontae Lee Williams*

"Death is not the greatest loss in life. The greatest loss is what dies inside us when we don't live."
-Norman Cousins

I am the b r o k e n c r a y o n

that can still create a MASTERPIECE, a master PEACE.

Each f r a c t u r e

a work of art
a working heart
still finding a way *to draw the perfect picture.*

distrACTION

So Nigeria really isn't happening. The Golden Globes get more attention than these tragedies. The game of distraction is sickening to watch play out, but it is a clear representation that attention is
boxed in and controlled
based on television/social media trends. It directs the flow of conversation, making certain conversations seem far more important than others. Meanwhile so many vitally important conversations barely receive any awareness or coverage at all.

For the Fallen

They are buried brick	crumbling walls don't speak well	they've mastered the sound of silence	tucked their hearts	close to lung held voice hostage

trapped in throats	thoughts in a labyrinth	manufactured maze of chaos	dilapidated conversation conjured in a speechless thunderstorm	dehydrated dungeons

where the air feeds us	borrowed art forms of silence	the high note of heaven is a chokehold	handcuffed nightmare spare tire	burning babylon with no destination

smoke and mirrors	shattered like pure innocence tweaking truth and geometric melanin telegram	phone me home	telepathic test-tube

holding time	like a body in the wind	like a caged song of sin	like a lyrical lie	tied tongue in knots

forgot the plot of rock and roll	cold souls trying to see the power of gravity	the power of gravity creating tragedy	when	you're	falling...

Sometimes you are the better composer. Not the better singer. The better writer. Not the better artist.

Execute

Working on execution and not just consistency.
Don't want to be passionately attached to my past with story after
story more than I'm passionately entrenched in the vision I have in
the present moment. I'm moving forward.

All this beautiful searching for a soul that refuses to see their own
beauty will leave us shipwrecked in a sea of insecurity.

You cannot snatch my halo.
You cannot snatch my heart.
You cannot dirty my spirit and handicap my soul from reaching its
fullest capacity.

When they steal your joy. They steal your happiness.
They steal your yearning to be in your body. They steal your true
essence for life.

The easiest way to destroy a human being's spirit
is to snatch their hope and their inspiration.
Joy is revolutionary.

The Meal Inside

Ode to the food desert

The brown paper bag became almost see through, as our fingerprints walked around it from securing the meal inside. It was four chicken wings and french fries. Both drenched in a world of ketchup and hot sauce. The sky was midnight heavy and the sirens in the hood were blaring like a soundtrack of chaos welcoming comfort. I recall my aunt saying *"I couldn't live in the city, it's too much violence."* My response, *"I couldn't live in the country, it's too much silence."* There is something about *city folk* that appreciates the loud noise and the unpredictability of violence and conflict.

We walked Broad Street a little after 12am smiling, discussing the girls we had crushes on and the ones that reminded us of boogies. Yes boogies! The ones that clinged on to you, but you never wanted to touch them!

The cement pavement littered with loose fast food sandwich wrappers everywhere and shattered broken glass, reflecting a glimmer from the streetlights. It looked like the shine of the night was having a conversation with our eyes.

We smiled and walked. We laughed and cracked jokes on one another with no interest in the noise around us. We were in our own world built of grease soaked fingers that continuously threw chicken bones to the ground as if ritual couldn't have sounded better. We washed down the french fries with our favorite sodas. Usually a coke that would give us a smile. And sometimes a *Tahitian Treat.*

Yes! We licked the satisfaction from our fingers while standing at a traffic light wondering why it tasted so **damn** good.

Expand

Everyone cannot be an evangelist of your thinking. It is impossible because there are so many different directions of thought and purpose flowing through this dimension. Being open to disagreement and still agreeing to unconditionally love someone is tough, but in these days and times, it is a necessity. Until we learn to embrace that way of thinking we will see more separation and conflict while walking this path of life.

We argue over ideas that are sacred ideologies of people that walked before us. We adopt and stand in those narratives and then live our lives through those story lines. It is interesting but we have to learn to love one another past ideology, philosophy and personal beliefs. We have to learn how to love unconditionally. We have to redefine what safe spaces mean. This is not easy, but as the world evolves, more changes will be coming. I pray we can act in love and not in the shaming and guilting of others. Yes there is a wrong and a right. A prolific model of expectation and standard that is needed to exist in the most healthy ways possible. But it will take dialogue, honest dialogue in a safe space where people are not so invested in protecting their bag of identity, but their core truth.

How much of you is really you and why do you identify with the world and your community the way you do?

What narrative are you behaving and performing and how much of it is really you?

Questions I've been pondering lately. Being open minded, healthy communication skills, the art of empathy and sensitivity are going to be well-needed skill sets in the now. We are already here. If truth is the light and someone shows you truth please do not run from it no matter how uncomfortable it might get. There is growth in leaving the comfort zone. Expand your mind and expand your soul.

No Complaints

Yesterday while doing yoga. A foot was ten inches from my face. It smelled like sweaty toes yelling Hallelujah!

I thought, "**don't complain**, a friend just transitioned from cancer. You're in pigeon pose still breathing, practicing stillness and breath control."

We know how to complain so well.

MJ Harris spoke of spending more time with family and friends. The truth of how we speak so much about our ambitions and grinding that we never really spend time to learn about the people who really matter. He really didn't complain a lot when he got sick. He faced it head on, practiced faith and kept his **heart and mind** open. He laughed and joked about it. Even if he was afraid you really wouldn't know it. He didn't pity himself. He did the things he loved like eat cheesesteaks and take in theatre. He fought and fought some more! He was **transparent and unafraid** to document his experience whether it was on Facebook or Vlogs. His music will love on forever and his words will live on forever. His light will live through us. That's legacy. I wonder if he is still questioning the play calls of football teams, the politics around music and theatre as a modern day thespian. Yes you will be missed, but your spirit will live on. I will write more. Eventually I will. Everyone take care of yourself and your soul. Feed it healthy food and energy..

Rest in Freedom MJ Harris

No Limits

No they cannot stop banging on the tables in the classroom
because the music is tired of being incarcerated
by the education system.

Besides
you are boring them with a redundant curriculum that is created

to box
in their
genius.

So stop trying to separate them from their authenticity and truth.

They are afraid of becoming the teacher/person
that lives a life with only a fraction of their truth, identity, and
potential.

The music inside of them
doesn't know limitations
until you decide to show them
what limits look like.

Open Letter 7

*When a person isn't secure with themselves
then you can never make them feel safe enough to be loved.*

Dear YOU

Never apologize for being a great person with big dreams.

An amazing vision.

A huge heart.

The world needs your best and if your best makes others insecure then so be it!

Never dim your light to be mediocre.

You are made in the reflection of God and God is not mediocre!

If you want a meaningful relationship you have to commit to something meaningful.
Something that breeds fulfillment. There is a big difference between complacency and fulfillment. When you commit to something that gives life instead of stagnancy
then you can grow. This isn't just with people but with self.
Our habits of how we relate to food, music, creativity, wealth, and much more.

Famous people get told "they love you" all the time by people who live life vicariously through them. That love is based on what they do for them. Such is the detachment. Fame is scary.

Open Letter 8: Two Too Many Toos

Two people on a date.
Two chairs. One Table.
Two Meals. Two phones.
Two x Two hands typing away.
Two sends per Two Seconds.
Two Facebook Pages.
Two Instagrams.
Two Twitter Handles.
Too Preoccupied.
Two Wants.
Too Dressed Up.
Too busy to notice.
One check.
One distorted reality.
No Connection. Too many distractions. Too bad.

- Bunmi Samuel

Someone

Lady,
Take my last name
Diamond rings on third fingers
Don't make the soul bling bling
True love was never defined by materialistic things
You are the other half I've been searching for
Mirror above my soul's dresser drawer
The reflection that completes me
Can I live inside your lungs
So you can breathe me
Can I lay on top of your tongue
So you can speak me
Can I run around inside of your eyelids
Looking for pictures of our future kids
So you can blink me
Can I sleep inside your mind
So you can think me
Drink me   Hold me   Console me   Unfold me
Like writing love letters in the back of a fifth grade classroom
Together me and you will create this album called infinity
Better yet
Let's create a song called eternity
God took my rib from me and gave it to you
So you would never have to lose faith in me
We are connected spiritually
Walking on the same brain waves mentally
So when I'm thinking of you
You're thinking of me
When I'm dreaming of you
You're dreaming of me
And we all want that someone
Someone to walk hand in hand with through life
Someone to hold
Who's special
Conversations special

So special you think you're talking to god
Someone to wake up next to in the morning
When it's real
No makeup on
Nothing fake at all
Just morning breathe
Boogies in eyes
Dried saliva on chin
And morning breathe is what you bathe in
That someone
That someone who will criticize you constructively
And simultaneously
Build you up into the pyramid you are instead of the project that
has been knocked down
You are not an object at all
This is beautiful
Just the shooting star that you can catch in your hands
And hold onto your wishes so when you hug them
It feels like your dreams are coming true
Yes that someone
That someone
So can I live inside your lungs
So you can breathe me
Can I lay on top of your tongue
So you can speak me
Can I run around inside your eyelids
Looking for pictures of our future kids
So you can blink me
Can I sleep inside your mind
So you can think me
Can i run around inside your arteries
til' I fall asleep on your heartbeat
So you can bleed me
I need you to need me
Cuz' we all need that someone

Screen Time

In a world of darkness the glowing screen becomes the guiding light. The shine provides chalk lines around the eyes of an entire generation erasing the vision within. Influence has become the drug of choice, an optical illusion mixed with ear pollution, false personas drowning in sound waves of normalized chaos. What will we make of this new nothing, a dark void causing a spiritual depression, drenching a blanket of cognitive fatigue over the masses. A populous growing delusional, attention addicts craving another hit of social capital, only to realize the day has arrived when they will have to pay to play in the algorithm. What happens when the concept of fame dies? When the idea of celebrity is no longer oxygen for the ego? The algorithm, an ocean of possibility keeping shadows from their owners, tricking them into a pursuit for a treasure chest. Jewels in the form of approval shining from their pages that delete their authenticity in order to conform to the opinionated shape shift of others ideas of what life should look like. Where is freedom when your personality is controlled by what others think? Humans have become sound bytes inside an echo chamber, imprisoned inside the cells of their cells, prisms that the digital age has provided. This is the new dope, I mean the means of approval ratings leads to obese checks and balance is blasphemy. The new business model is built on a grind that will chew the brain stem until branches lynch memories of the past. Insomniacs with an early onset of alzheimers, forgetting to put the phone down, because they can't remember what life is like without a phone in their hands. In a world of darkness the glowing screen becomes the guiding light.

Impact Of Television

The world changed when media and entertainment moved from radio receivers to the television. When the television was invented it was sat in living rooms across the country, with the families surrounding the glowing screen waiting for something to appear. Families would sit in their living rooms staring at static screens with hopes that they would eventually see entertainment. This moved people's imaginations from a space of where they were able to generate their own sort of what the story lines were on radio receivers, to a place where the screen actually told them who people were both recently and religiously. Now people's conscious mind was actually being told what a storyline and setting was. This cultivated images in peoples minds, causing their imagination to be programmed, cultivated by whomever or whatever controlled the sources of information that came through the screen.

The Dopamine Generation

A society obsessed with the dopamine hit,

the chemical that creates the feeling of euphoria,

will eventually crash, because of its obsession

with happiness.

A happiness addiction so strong that people are willing

to consume or do anything to induce a state of artificial joy

during dark times.

A magic spell of darkness where people speak depression into existence

by claiming it over their spirit.

Now this is not to negate the chemical challenges with serotonin

(naturally produced dopamine)

but one must ask if the lack of emotional vocabulary and intelligence

is a reason behind internalizing the concept of depression.

Marriage Anniversary

It's our ANNIVERSARY!

I can't believe it's been a year! Here are some lessons from marriage.

Marriage has shown the continuous process of working on oneself is a never ending journey. *When you are doing marriage or a relationship correctly there is nowhere to hide. Your partner will serve as a mirror.*

My Wife has been my reflection of evaluation, introspection, awareness and much more. Her words of accountability, motivation, and truth have been a stimulating **growth plan**. I pray each day I'm able to return the favor with the same focus, capacity, and that she does. At a certain point I was running from myself in each relationship I chartered territory into. I carved paths of trepidation, knowing love takes courage. For years I replicated messages from fear based narratives, inner-child wounds, and mixed messages from relationships around me. Immature habits and behaviors would rise to the surface for me to notice. Instead of taking notice, practicing awareness to intentionally work on them, I would ignore the need to work on myself.

Here's the truth! There is no hiding from yourself. There is no running. When you commit to marriage you're committing to reevaluating yourself on a daily basis, because your decisions directly impact another person. All the time. Marriage is a classroom where you're inspired to study. It takes a higher level of awareness in order to become the best version of yourself. It is not just for you, but for your partner in life. And when they arrive they revive the labor, the work it takes to evolve. Thank you to my wife for supporting me as I amplify this search and journey of self through our son, her and I. Happy Anniversary.

Acknowledgements

First and foremost I would like to thank the Most High God for providing this abundant blessing called life. Thank you for oxygen and the art of breathing. For teaching me the power of giving. For en(light)ening me with electricity to write on a frequency of limitless possibility. For teaching me how to be solar system in a world of planets that forgot how to be universe. **I thank you. Thank you.**

The highest praise and gratitude goes to my Mother, Donna and Father, Greg Sr for bringing me into this world, and raising me into the sunshine I've become. Without your shine, there is no flame inside of me. You made me everything I am and then some. **I thank you. Thank you.**

To my sisters Dyisha, Donna, and Bernissa, thank you for always supporting me, having my back and being ready to, y'all know the rest. **I thank you. Thank you.**

To my lovely Wife Helanah, thank you for being a laser beam of inspiration, reminding me of what I'm capable of, saying yes to me and all my wacky genius ways. As well as inspiring me to stretch, grow and work towards completion. **I thank you. Thank you.**

To my son Noble Sage, you are the reminder of legacy, the seed of infinite impact. You have taught me so much already, and I look forward to more lessons as you grow and grow us. **I thank you. Thank you.**

To my closest friends and family. You know who you are. I love you. Thank you for reminding me why I'm here and where my roots are. You've taught me to grow my branches fearlessly. No matter the soil, I will bloom. **I thank you. Thank you.**

To every educator, writing coach, and mentor that has ignited, encouraged, and inspired me to have faith in my abilities as an effective communicator whether verbal or written. You shifted my paradigm as a thinker, writer and human. **I thank you. Thank you.**

To the editor of Breathing Ashes, Scott Raven Tarazevits. Thank you for your support, guidance, and patience as I moved through this process. **I thank you. Thank you.**

To my multiple poetry squads GhettoHero SupaMan Savapoets (Jonifin Marvin and Don Carlos), Synthesized Minds (Will Wright, BJ, and Les), and Just US (Kevin White, Rell, and Adam) thank you for expanding my artistic potential, sharpening my skills with healthy challenge and competition. Our group poems kept me going! Thank you for brotherhood and fellowship. To all the open mic poetry spots and my peers across the world, **I thank you. Thank you.**

To all the youth poets I've had the pleasure to work with, coach and mentor, thank you for showing me purpose. Witnessing your evolution and impact in the world allows me to see my endless potential of possibility, and the superpower of imagination. Continue to write life into existence. I would say names, but you know who you are. One of my biggest inspirations. Love. **I thank you. Thank you.**

To my inspirations: There are truly too many to name. To every writer, songwriter, journalist, comic, painter, dancer, musician, magician, sculptor, speaker and so on. Your electricity is contagious. **I thank you. Thank you.**

To the elders still here and those who have left. Your spirit lives beyond your flesh. You are the foundation that holds us up. **I thank you. Thank you.**

To YOU, thank you for your support. For spending time with me and allowing me to share my journey with you. It is a blessing that I hold dear to my heart. I am humbled. Thank you for taking this walk with me and following whatever sent you my way. I am supported. Thank you for reading that piece to your friend from page X and re-reading that piece with your favorite underlined lines on page X. I pray the magic of these words expands your imagination, your wildest wonders, your heart and your world. **I thank you. Thank you.**

Thank you.

GET LOST IN YOUR WONDER.
CURIOSITY IS KEY.
IT IS YOUR MAGIC.

@GregCorbinSpeaks

(BUY THE T-SHIRT)

Works Cited

2pac-T.H.U.G.L.I.F.E.(The Hate U Give Little Infants Fuck Everybody). - YouTube. https://www.youtube.com/watch?v=QCEf557fNYg. Accessed 4 Feb. 2021.

Bach, Richard. *The Bridge Across Forever: A True Love Story*. William Morrow, 1982.

Butler, Octavia E. *Parable of the Talents*. Seven Stories Press, 1998.

Cohen, Leonard. "Anthem." *The Future*, Columbia, 1992.

hooks, bell. *All About Love: New Visions*. William Morrow, 1999.

Laird, Sam. "Stuart Scott: Cool as the Other Side of the Pillow."*Mashable*, 4 Jan. 2015, https://mashable.com/2015/01/04/stuart-scott-legacy/.

Lyubovny, Vlad. *Khalil Kain Says Tupac Became "2Pac" After His Role As Bishop in 'Juice' (Part 5) - YouTube*. 27 Apr. 2018, https://www.youtube.com/watch?v=hw0mS-v3LIU.

Pollett, Bill. "We Are Not Made of Atoms." *The Voice Magazine*, 26 Aug. 2005, https://www.voicemagazine.org/2005/08/26/we-are-not-made-of-atoms/.

"Quote by Marianne Williamson." *Goodreads*, https://www.goodreads.com/quotes/387102-something-amazing-happens-when-we-surrender-and-just-love-we. Accessed 4 Feb. 2021.

Regan, Lilith. *Quotes by Carl Jung: The Complete Collection ofOver 100 Quotes*. Independently Published, 2020.

About The Author

Executive Leadership Coach, Professional Speaker, Poet, Storyteller, and Imagination Activist, Greg Corbin II has built his career by listening to the needs of the culture and preparing us for it. He is focused on creating spaces of authentic human connection because he knows this is how we win as a community, leaving no one behind. Just out of college, Corbin grew a small idea into a leading grassroots nonprofit impacting 50,000+ youth in just 10 years. He became a highly sought-after thought-partner for large organizations such as HBO, CNN, The Aspen Institute and YouthSpeaks, later co-founding Brainchild Inspiration Group. Corbin has performed sharing stages with Sonia Sanchez, Nikki Giovanni, Mos Def, Talib Kweli, Tobe Nwigwe, Michael Eric Dyson, Tank and the Bangas, Black Thought, Charlamagne Da God and India Aire. Connect with him at GregCorbinSpeaks@gmail.com.

Made in the USA
Columbia, SC
20 August 2022